Jorge Luis Borges

CRITICAL STUDIES IN
LATIN AMERICAN CULTURE

SERIES EDITORS:

James Dunkerley
Jean Franco
John King

This major series — the first of its kind to appear in English — is designed to map the field of contemporary Latin American culture, which has enjoyed increasing popularity in Britain and the United States in recent years.

Six titles will offer a critical introduction to twentieth-century developments in painting, poetry, music, fiction, cinema and 'popular culture'. Further volumes will explore more specialized areas of interest within the field.

The series aims to broaden the scope of criticism of Latin American culture, which tends still to extol the virtues of a few established 'master' works and to examine cultural production within the context of twentieth-century history. These clear, accessible studies are aimed at those who wish to know more about some of the most important and influential cultural works and movements of our time.

Other Titles in the Series

DRAWING THE LINE: ART AND CULTURAL IDENTITY IN CONTEMPORARY LATIN AMERICA by Oriana Baddeley and Valerie Fraser

PLOTTING WOMEN: GENDER AND REPRESENTATION IN MEXICO by Jean Franco

JOURNEYS THROUGH THE LABYRINTH: LATIN AMERICAN FICTION IN THE TWENTIETH CENTURY by Gerald Martin

MAGICAL REELS: A HISTORY OF CINEMA IN LATIN AMERICA by John King

MEMORY AND MODERNITY: POPULAR CULTURE IN LATIN AMERICA by William Rowe and Vivian Schelling

MISPLACED IDEAS: ESSAYS ON BRAZILIAN CULTURE by Roberto Schwarz

THE GATHERING OF VOICES: THE TWENTIETH-CENTURY POETRY OF LATIN AMERICA by Mike Gonzalez and David Treece

Jorge Luis Borges

A Writer on the Edge

◆

BEATRIZ SARLO

Edited by John King

VERSO

London · New York

First published by Verso, in association with the Centre of Latin American Studies
at the University of Cambridge, 1993
© Verso 1993
All rights reserved

Verso
UK: 6 Meard Street, London W1V 3HR
USA: 29 West 35th Street, New York, NY 10001-2291

Verso is the imprint of New Left Books

ISBN 0-86091-440-2
ISBN 0-86091-635-9 (pbk)

British Library Cataloguing in Publication Data
A catalogue record for this book is available from the British Library

Library of Congress Cataloging-in-Publication Data
A catalogue record for this book is available from the Library of Congress

Typeset in Perpetua by Leaper & Gard Ltd, Bristol
Printed in Great Britain by Biddles Ltd, Guildford, Surrey

Contents

Editor's Preface

I

In September 1973, I met Borges in his flat in downtown Buenos Aires. I had travelled to Argentina to interview his great friend the writer Adolfo Bioy Casares, whom I had first encountered in a Borges story, 'Tlön, Uqbar, Orbis Tertius'. Bioy, however, was spending a couple of months in France, so I went in search of his group of friends.

The route to Borges's house took me across a city teeming with flags, rallies and bands. Perón had recently returned, after eighteen years in exile, and everyone, it seemed, was claiming him as their own. It took time to cross Corrientes Street, since a huge Peronist youth demonstration was leaping down that main thoroughfare to the beat of hundreds of drums. The walls were covered in slogans and posters. The image of Evita was everywhere, even though she had been dead for twenty years and Perón was returning with a much younger wife, Isabelita. Students in the university asked me why I wanted to see Borges: what relevance did his elitist, escapist fantasies have in this world of political mobilization? A decade later the Argentine sociologist Silvia Sigal commented on the reception of Borges in these years. A writer, Jorge Feinman, had told her that 'at the beginning of the 1970s, I liked Borges, but I said so under my breath'. And David Viñas, the critic and writer, had replied to Sigal's question as to who was the most important creator or intellectual in Argentina in the last twenty years with a *boutade*: 'Borges, hélas!'[1]

Borges was one of the few not out on the street. He viewed the return of Perón as a further cyclical eruption of that populist madness which periodically stained Argentine society. He would write a year or so later, in his preface to *The Book of Sand* (1975):

> I do not write for a select minority, which means nothing to me, nor for that adulated platonic entity known as 'The Masses'. Both abstractions, so dear to the demagogue, I disbelieve in. I write for myself and for my friends, and I write to ease the passing of time.[2]

In his rather spartan flat, Borges directed me to the bookshelf where his favourite — English — works of literature were to be found. As he searched for the book that I would have to read to him — few English speakers escaped from Borges's flat without reading to him, although he usually took over the recital, quoting whole poems or passages of prose from memory — he told me of a recent experience he had suffered. There was no way of knowing if the story was true or apocryphal — Borges had been making up stories for foreign visitors or the local press ever since, in the early 1960s, he became the focus of constant media attention. One local journalist had asked him, he said, what he thought of Perón. He had answered by asking how Perón had kept alive for so many years in exile in Spain: perhaps he had given Spanish lessons. (This is a variation of an old joke, which Sarlo explains in Chapter 7: Borges was as scathing of the Spaniards' claim to linguistic purity as he was of Perón's demagogic manipulation and perversion of genuine River Plate Spanish.) The journalist had not seen the joke and reported him in sensationalist tones — *Borges Speaks Out Against Perón!* A week later Borges had travelled to La Plata to give a lecture, but this was cancelled, because someone had put a bomb under the dais. When he recalled, or invented, the bomb incident, his voice shook with rage. 'What cowards they were, to try to kill me that way — me, a blind old man! Why didn't they come at me with a gun, or better still with a knife?' Here in his library, ambiguously sheltered from the noise outside, Borges dreamt of meeting his American destiny — like so many of his characters — in a criollo duel, in the thrust of a knife. Here this guru of European and North American literary critics, hailed as one of the great writers of the twentieth century, was for a time trapped and lonely in the city he loved — ignored or, in his terms, menaced by his compatriots, imagining a heroic destiny that linked him to his nineteenth-century military ancestors or to elemental gaucho violence. It was a confusing meeting:

how was one to read Borges, what was his place as a writer, as an intellectual, in both Argentina and in Europe — the two traditions he claimed as his own?

Seven years later, in 1980, the dystopia that Borges had evoked at Perón's return seemed to have become a reality, though not in the way that Borges had envisaged. Perón had returned, governed for several months, and then died. His wife Isabel, surrounded by a motley crew of advisers, had taken over the government, and violence and disorder had spiralled almost out of control. The internecine struggle had already claimed many lives and forced thousands into exile before the military took over in March 1976. Those who, like Borges, thought that the military would clean up the political mess and then retire, leaving a stable political structure in place, were soon savagely disabused. The military had its own agenda: to extirpate the 'cancer' of political unrest and social mobilization by abolishing politics and waging a violent offensive against its actual or perceived enemies. Many thousands died and hundreds of thousands fled into exile in this campaign which fractured society and the intellectual field.

I had come to Buenos Aires, at a time when the military were beginning to lose their absolute authority, to study an Arts Centre, the Di Tella, which had been the focus of 'swinging Buenos Aires' in the 1960s. It still seemed a particularly inappropriate moment to be looking at a period of cultural and political ferment since this ferment had been brutally suppressed, but I found a number of artists and intellectuals who had been the protagonists of the sixties, also considering the same questions, as part of what Sarlo would later term a 'collective auto-biography'.[3] I met Beatriz Sarlo together with her friends and colleagues, the artist Juan Pablo Renzi and the critics María Teresa Gramuglio and Carlos Altamirano. These people, along with a number of other critics and artists, had organized reading groups in their houses as part of a 'catacomb' culture, an attempt to keep intellectual debate alive at a time when the universities and all forms of cultural diffusion were under strict military censorship, condemning a generation of young people to grow up in an intellectual void.

They had begun to publish a cultural journal, *Punto de Vista*, to test the limits of what could be discussed openly or indirectly in that period. (Significantly, early articles offered a revision of Argentine literary history and a reappraisal of writers such as Borges.) At a memorable dinner which began sedately but then raged throughout the night, they started off discussing my research topic and then began to question the meaning of the sixties and early seventies in Argentina, that elusive search to bring together the political and cultural vanguards. They explored the limitations of populist nationalism, of theoretical models, from Che to Mao, from Althusser to Lacan. They discussed the hopes and aspirations of a generation which had seemingly been dashed in the mid seventies and speculated on the way forward, the attempt to reconstruct a fragmented intellectual field, both at home and in exile. These were the tasks of the 1980s, as Argentina returned slowly to democracy. This book, some ten years later, is the result of such thoughtful rethinking and rewriting of a tradition. Because Borges is the most significant writer in twentieth-century Argentina, and a writer that eludes neat categorization, to come to terms with his *oeuvre* is one of the most important challenges for the Argentine critic.

II

It is a challenge that few critics have answered in a satisfactory way. In fact, a reading of criticism on Borges allows one to map with some precision the developing intellectual field in twentieth-century Argentina.[4] Borges played a most active role in the avant-garde movements of the 1920s in Argentina, as Chapters 7 and 8 of this book reveal. It was the task of this group to carve out a new space for itself in opposition both to the grand old men of Argentine culture, as represented by Leopoldo Lugones, and to the naturalist and socially committed work of other young writers. To support 'the new', they claimed, was in itself a revolutionary activity. Any criticism of Borges, therefore, would come from those opposed to the self-assertiveness of the youthful vanguard. The different groups traded insults and Borges's caustic, lapidary statements gave a fine cutting edge to these debates. The recognition that Borges was at the forefront of literary experimentation would last until well into the 1930s. The French writer Pierre Drieu la Rochelle commented memorably in 1933, on a visit to Buenos Aires, that 'Borges vaut le voyage'. It was only in the late 1930s, when Borges began to write the short stories that would later bring him worldwide fame, that the intellectual field began to line up in terms of different political ideologies and that the debates about cultural nationalism, which, as Sarlo explains in Chapter 7, had been prominent throughout the first decades of the century, received a new inflection.

By the 1930s, the liberal patrician order that had overseen the spectacular economic development of the Argentine from the 1880s to the 1920s — an order which was Borges's 'family' tradition — was entering crisis. Slowly a critique of elite, liberal European values began to emerge; more populist, narrowly nationalist political groupings came onto the scene, and under Perón, in the elections of 1946, they gained power. In these new readings, writers such as Borges could be crudely portrayed as lackeys of a system that had allowed a landowning elite and foreign interest groups to distort Argentine development. For a time, however, such ideas had little or no resonance in the wider society. Borges's revolutionary short stories of the late thirties and early forties — his most productive period since the mid 1920s — were supported by an influential group of writers and critics. His popularity was clearly not widespread since, as Sarlo shows, he offered a radical break with the dominant traditions of psychological realism, costumbrism and naturalism. His work demanded new readers who, as his friend Bioy Casares pointed out in an early review, were almost 'specialists in litera-ture'. But writers and intellectuals, in the main, supported his work and many fell under his spell, in Argentina and gradually throughout Latin America. The novelists and poets who came into prominence in the 1960s — Julio Cortázar, Octavio Paz, Gabriel García Márquez, José Donoso, Carlos Fuentes and Mario Vargas Llosa amongst others were profoundly influenced by Borges.

Witold Gombrowicz, the Polish writer, had remained in Argentina throughout the Second World War. It is reported that when he finally left Buenos Aires for Europe, he shouted down from the boat to his friends on the quay 'Jóvenes, matad a Borges' ('Young people kill Borges'). He realized that Borges had become the dominant force in the literary system and that new generations would have to come to terms with, or write against, his influence. A number of critics took his words perhaps over-literally. At a time when Borges was enthralling young writers throughout Latin America and was gradually becoming known in France (the first translations into French date from the mid-1940s) and later in the English-speaking world, young critics began to engage in the patricide hinted at by Gombrowicz. The criticisms varied in complexity. At the crudest, he fell victim to an anti-imperialist populism, fuelled by the diffuse nationalist rhetoric of the first Perón regime (1946-1955).

His stories were seen as elitist evasions from the 'real', his heterodox views on foreign influences were interpreted as *extranjerizante* (foreign-loving, at the expense of the nation). Critics such as Arturo Jauretche, Jorge Aberlardo Ramos and Juan José Hernández Arregui were harbingers of the new brutalism.

Young critics at the University of Buenos Aires, known, after the title of their literary magazine, as the *Contorno* group, tried to avoid such populist excesses, but were still conscious that Borges represented, for them, an order and a class that had to be blown away by the winds of modernity. There is a paradox in the fact that at a time when *Les Temps Modernes* began to publish Borges, Sartre was deployed in Argentina to teach the necessity of commitment. Since Borges was not overtly committed, he felt the barbs of critics such as Adolfo Prieto, who in 1954 wrote a book called *Borges and the New Generation*.[5] This essay is interesting only in so far as it reveals the blind spot that critics demonstrated when trying to deal with Borges. The work of *Contorno* was in the main quite subtle and complex in its revision of literary and political traditions and its relation of literary texts to their context. But Borges did not fit into any easy category and he was explained away in a series of rather banal observations such as 'wit, erudition and an excellent style do not ensure great literature'; his essays, his poetry and his prose were mere *divertissements*, not appropriate to the serious tasks facing young people. The *Contorno* group were the teachers of Beatriz Sarlo's generation, and it would take the work of her contemporaries to explore this blind spot or correct what Sarlo has called *Contorno*'s *estrabismo literario*, or 'literary squint'.[6]

The downfall of Perón in 1955 heralded a decade or more of modernization in the intellectual field in Argentina. After the cultural autarky of those years, Argentina was once again receptive to 'the new'. The sixties were a time of political and cultural ferment. A student or young intellectual in that decade — and this is the generation of Beatriz Sarlo — would be receptive to different influences. The political realm was becoming ever more radicalized. Perón and Peronism, in a curious but understandable sleight of hand, were reconsidered as potential leaders of a Third-World, nationalist, socialist consciousness. The Cuban Revolution, the influence of Mao, the impact of the Vietnam War, the radicalization of May 1968 all had their echoes in Argentina. These processes had their intellectual mentors: first Sartre — but then also Althusser, Foucault and Lacan (the first translations of Althusser and

Lacan appeared within months of the books appearing in France: Argentines have always been avid readers of theory). More generally, there was an increase in consumerism, not just of goods, but of many different aspects of culture. This was a time in which considerable sums were spent on advertising, visits to the psychoanalyst became an integral part of middle-class Buenos Aires life, people flocked to the films of Ingmar Berman and helped create a 'boom' in Latin American fiction by buying novels by the tens of thousands. Borges, who in the 1920s and 1930s had always joked that he gave his books away since no one bought them, now found that he had a large and ever-expanding audience at home. Weekly journals grew up to reflect and direct these new tastes, and fashion in all its aspects became extremely important. Borges was at the forefront of journalists' attention and he took to this new fame with mocking glee. Indeed, he became for some sectors an icon of the 1960s. When the journal *Primera Plana* printed a map of 'swinging' Buenos Aires in the 1960s, putting in all the fashionable bars, galleries, cinemas and restaurants, 'Georgie's' house was marked alongside the arts centres and the galleries.

Critical attention to Borges might have been expected to echo his new 'star' status. After all, fashionable French structuralists and post-structuralists from Foucault to Genette to Todorov were all quoting him and he was a campus attraction throughout the United States. Film directors paid homage to him, philosophers played with his paradoxes. To a certain extent critics in Argentina followed these modern readings for, as Sarlo points out, Borges's writings seemed to reflect or anticipate current critical concerns to do with intertextuality, the referential illusion or the 'death of the author'.

Yet he still remained a problem for those who wished to see him as an 'Argentine' writer commenting, however obliquely, on Argentine traditions and life. The Left, the nationalists and the populists (and these categories include a whole gamut of overlapping and interlocking concerns) continued to be deeply suspicious of him. Borges himself scarcely helped them by embracing a series of distinctly unfashionable political causes. He hated Perón, he opposed the Cuban Revolution, he spoke out in favour of the abortive Bay of Pigs invasion, he supported the Argentine Conservative party, he accepted a medal of honour from the Chilean dictator Pinochet within months of the bloody coup in Chile. None of these choices commended him to an increasingly radicalized young generation that could only read his work in terms of the persuasive rhetorics of class, dependency, underdevelopment and Third Worldism. In such a world of committed 'truths', he was at best an anachronism and at worst the cultural lackey of neo-imperialist powers. The political and the cultural vanguards were in this sense drifting far apart or rather, as Sarlo puts it, 'the young leftist scholars and intellectuals of the first part of the seventies had thought in terms of a strong subordination (much stronger than the term hegemony conveys) of culture to politics, of experience to theory, of the popular world to political parties organized according to a Leninist model'.[7] Althusser had argued for a leading role for intellectuals in revolutionary theory, while Foucault (who in another paradox was at the same time a sophisticated reader of Borges, as witness introduction to *The Order of Things*) and his analysis of knowledge and power, 'had a strong and persuasive effect on the mentality of the young, who felt no inclination for reformism and wanted to submit their practices to the public validation of politics'.[8] Foucault on power was understandable; Foucault on Borges was left aside. Winning the day was the important point, establishing the utopia of social change. Few saw that Borges had warned in his stories, written in the early forties, of utopian orders that collapsed into dystopia. Such was the case of Argentina in the 1970s. The brutal military dictatorship of 1976 would cause the fractured intellectual field to rethink its basic premises and reconstruct new models. Beatriz Sarlo has been central in this process.

III

Although some of Sarlo's early writings appeared in the late sixties and early seventies, her most important work dates from the late 1970s. Since 1978 she has directed the cultural magazine *Punto de Vista* which is today the most important journal of socialist theory in Argentina. Like all the best little magazines, it is sustained by a common project and a close-knit group of contributors: Carlos Altamirano, María Teresa Gramuglio, Juan Carlos Pontiero, Sarlo herself, Hilda Sábato, Hugo Vezzetti, Oscar Terán, Rafael Felipelli and others. In its pages we read the response of socialist critics to the political issues of the day: the breakup of the military dictorship, the futility of the Falklands/Malvinas war, the difficulties faced by President Alfonsín's new democratic order, and the shame of the government pardoning of the military leaders who had overseen campaigns of murder. The magazine has recently charted the cartwheels and pirouettes of Menem's conservative populism, a Thatcherite Peronist to use an oxymoron worthy of Borges (although Borges did not live long enough to witness this new-style Peronism). *Punto de Vista* has also charted the shifts in cultural theory, from the demise of structuralist Marxism through the contemporary debates about modernity and postmodernity. British historians and critics such as Perry Anderson, E.P. Thompson and Raymond Williams have been presented to Argentine readers alongside continental European critics and Latin American theorists. On several occasions Sarlo and others have pointed to the particular usefulness of Raymond Williams's work as a way of reconceptualizing the cultural field. While structuralism and structuralist Marxism had seen 'experience' as a dirty word, part of vulgar materialism or historicism, in this new climate in Argentina, an analysis of 'lived experience' or 'structures of feeling', forms of practical consciousness, seemed to open up new possibilities. Williams also showed that the history of words could open up new areas of semantic and historical analysis. As Sarlo puts it,

> We had our own key words to explore. For example, the words gaucho, gringo, criollo, barbarian, immigrant, which formed a sequence that ran through the second half of the nineteenth century into the first decades of the twentieth. The processes of resemantization that Williams explored provided a frame that could be translated into our own questions about the cultural constitution of Argentina.[9]

Rereading Argentine culture through Williams and through Gramsci, amongst others, allowed the magazine to undertake a radical rewriting of Argentine history and a thorough critique of what they termed the 'simplistic versions of history', in particular the orthodoxies of populist nationalism and dependency theory.

Sarlo's many articles in *Punto de Vista* and her series of books open up new possibilities for readings, rather than offering yet more theoretical models or critical paradigms.[10] Her first major book of the 1980s, written with Carlos Altamirano, took a fresh look at Argentine cultural history, from the mid-nineteenth century. Chapter 7 below is taken from this early work, *Ensayos argentinos: de Sarmiento a la vanguardia* (Argentine Essays: from Sarmiento to the Avant-Garde, 1983). Together with Altamirano she wrote a critical guide to literary and cultural theory, *Literatura/Sociedad* (Literature/Society, 1983) — a comprehensive introduction to the topic combining European and North American theorists with the most incisive Latin American critics and offering key readings of texts as *exempla* of a problematical field. All too quickly and all too early, they argue implicitly, Argentine critics have confused and collapsed badly thought-out political ideologies into the domain of cultural theory. What should we read, they ask — and *how* should we read?

From this point, Sarlo's own research has concentrated on the impact of modernity in Argentina, in particular in the 1920s. In this, she questions an essentialist strand of Latin American cultural history which sees the 'popular' as residing in rural or indigenous cultures. Here the key-word for Sarlo — and it is a word that is fundamental to this book on Borges — is cultural 'mixture', the bringing together of different layers of experience, urban and rural, Latin American and European, elite and popular. This 'mixture' would not be a simple blend — as a term such as 'melting-pot' might imply — but instead a locus of creative tensions. Sarlo expresses these views in trenchant fashion: 'I refuse to think of Argentine culture as an act of homogenization carried out in the name of national identity, or the working class, or the people (or whatever the political perspectives that the Left take up on these matters). Nor do I think that it is true to the facts to think of the history of this culture as an interminable battle between national and anti-national battalions. It is also inexact to see this process as a clear-cut choice between "progressive" and "reactionary" forces. Finally, another temptation that haunts the Left is that of missionary paternalism, which makes them try to save the popular sectors from the dangers of "high" and cosmopolitan culture and, in the name of a respect due to regional, rural or folk cultures, to celebrate in Panglossian style, something that is probably the result of inequalities, injustice and deprivation.'[11]

Her own work looks at the complex layering of these different cultural levels: from literature to art to journalism and to the *roman feuilleton*. She has published on women's magazines and serial literature: *El imperio de los sentimentos* (The Empire of Sentiment, 1985); and on modernity and Buenos Aires: *Una modernidad periférica: Buenos Aires 1920 y 1930* (A Peripheral Modernity: Buenos Aires 1920 and 1930, 1988). Chapters 1 and 8 of the present book are drawn in part from this recent brilliant and multifaceted work, which explores the impact of modernity on the city and its intellectuals, writers and artists. The central motif of 'modernity on the margins' runs through both the above-mentioned volumes. Most recently, in *La imaginación técnica* (The

Technical Imagination, 1992), she looks at the ways in which the modern dreams of technology (inventions, radio, mass communications) influenced different aspects of Argentine culture in the 1920s and 1930s. Her work is grounded on meticulous, close research which constantly engages with, but also keeps a lucid distance from, received ideas and canonical readings. In this way she decentres the dominant orthodoxies, be they structuralist, populist or postmodernist, and explores the space and freedom of the margins. As a result, she is an especially good reader of Borges.

IV

The present book brings together these different concerns. It grows out of a series of lectures given at Cambridge University in 1992 which concentrated on a close reading of certain of Borges's poems and short stories. It is framed (in Chapters 1, 7 and 8) by her research on the Argentine cultural field in the 1920s which, as she puts it, offers a land-scape for Borges, a context in which to read his work. She maps the deve-lopment of her argument in the Introduction, but it should be noted that Sarlo's purpose is at least twofold. She gives North American and Euro-pean readers a sense of Borges as writing within and against an Argentine tradition which is in itself a 'cosmopolitan' tradition. She also allows Latin American and in particular Argentine critics to correct the 'squint' imposed by tendentious readings, and to offer them new ways of seeing.

In true Borgesian fashion, this book is a tissue of different languages and translations. The Introduction and Chapters 7 and 8 were written in Spanish and translated by the editor. Chapter 1 was written in Spanish and translated by Jorge Myers, whose version the author amended slightly. Chapters 2–6 were conceived and written in English by the author, but intended for oral delivery at the University of Cambridge. Whilst the editors have made some corrections with a view to avoiding any major dissonances in these different registers, no sustained attempt has been made to iron out the oral tone of the bulk of the book. These were given as a lecture series and are here presented in that form. In Borges, as in Sarlo, each sentence contains complex ideas that need to be unravelled by the reader. This task may sometimes be very challenging, but it is always rewarding.

John King
University of Warwick

Notes

1. Silvia Sigal, *Intelectuales y poder en la década del sesenta*, Buenos Aires, 1991, p. 26.

2. J.L. Borges, *The Book of Sand*, London 1977, p. 2.

3. For Beatriz Sarlo's revision of the 1960s, see 'Intelectuales: escisión o mimesis', *Punto de Vista* 25, December 1985.

4. See María Luisa Bastos, *Borges ante la crítica argentina, 1923–1960*, Buenos Aires 1974.

5. Adolfo Prieto, *Borges y la nueva generación*, Buenos Aires, 1954, pp. 86-7.

6. Beatriz Sarlo, 'Los dos ojos de *Contorno*', *Punto de Vista* 13, November 1981, p. 7.

7. Beatriz Sarlo, 'Raymond Williams in Argentina', lecture given at King's College, Cambridge, April 1992, *mimeo*. To be published by the Centre of Latin American Studies in Cambridge.

8. Ibid.

9. Ibid.

10. Patricia D'Allemand makes this point in her excellent introduction to the work of Beatriz Sarlo, 'Hacia una crítica literaria latinoamericana: nacionalismo y cultura en el discurso de Beatriz Sarlo', Centre for Latin American Cultural Studies, King's College, London, Occasional Paper 1, 1990.

11. Beatriz Sarlo, 'La izquierda ante la cultura: del dogmatismo al populismo', *Punto de Vista* 20, May 1984, p. 25.

For Juan Pablo Renzi

Introduction

This book has grown out of four lectures that I gave at the University of Cambridge in February 1992 as the Simón Bolívar Professor of Latin American Studies. In giving these lectures on Borges I experienced a curious feeling. In a British university, an Argentine woman professor was talking about an Argentine writer who is today considered 'universal'. Indeed since those far-off years in the 1950s when translations of some of his work appeared in *Les Temps Modernes*, Borges has joined the small group of writers who are known throughout the world (more widely known than read, which is how fame works nowadays). Far from the climate which conditions the reading of his work in Argentina, and firmly established within Western literature, Borges has almost lost his nationality: he is stronger than Argentine literature itself, more powerful than the cultural tradition to which he belongs. If Balzac and Baudelaire or Dickens and Jane Austen seem inseparable from something that we can call 'French literature' or 'English literature', Borges, by contrast, moves in a world in which the term 'Argentine literature' is rarely heard.

There are many reasons for this, but here I would like to address what I consider to be the most important of them: in the current European climate, the image of Borges is more potent than that of Argentine literature. The fact is that in Europe Borges can be read without reference to the marginal region where he wrote all his work. In this way we are given a Borges who is explained by (and at the same time explains) Western culture and the versions that this culture also offers of the Orient, and not a Borges who is also explained by (and explains) Argentine culture, and particularly the culture of Buenos Aires. Borges's reputation in the world has cleansed him of nationality. Another contributing factor is without doubt the rare perfection that Borges's writing achieves in a language like English. We could argue that this language, English, is the language of his cultural roots or, if that statement seems too strong, it is certainly one of the strongest influences on him. Be that as it may, the lectures in Cambridge brought this image of Borges home to me — it was something I should have known before — and I received further verification when I found paperback editions of Borges, alongside ancient and modern classics, in every single bookshop that I visited in Britain. What I am saying is nothing new and could be put down to the surprise of an ingenuous provincial. However, I felt at the same time that something of Borges (at least of the Borges that we read in the city that he loved, Buenos Aires) was lost in this process of triumphant universalization. Reading Borges as a writer without nationality, as a great among the greats, is aesthetically totally justifiable: his work addresses the concerns, the questions, the myths that we in the West consider universal. But such a reading, however well justified, implies both recognition and loss, because Borges has gained what he always considered to be his — the right of Latin Americans to work within all traditions. He has also lost, albeit partially, something that he considered to be an essential part of his world: his links with River Plate cultural traditions and with nineteenth-century Argentina.

It is not a question of restoring Borges to a picturesque and folkloric world that he always rejected, but rather of allowing him to speak to the texts and to the authors with whom he engaged in literary polemics, restoring him to the context in which he made his aesthetic breaks. These authors do not all belong to the great canon of a universal tradition. They are often not well known, yet they were important in the cultural field that Borges participated in from the 1920s on.

The first chapters of this book explore what Borges made of the ineluctable fact of having been born in, and of writing in, Argentina. Hopefully, by this means, it will be possible to see with some clarity the ways in which Borges maintained a dialogue with Western culture. In the course of a few decades, Borges presented Argentina with a new and different way of relating to literature. He completely reorganized the system, placing at one end of it the residual gauchesque tradition and at the other end the fictionalization of the theory of the intertext, years before it was disseminated by books of literary criticism. For this reason,

Borges is a 'commonplace' for Argentine readers and writers, and his influence can be seen in a sort of lingua franca, a literary koine, in which the twists of his stories are mixed up with anecdotes that he himself mischievously invented for the mass media and repeated in hundreds of interviews from the 1960s onwards. It is easier today in Argentina to show that the question of Argentine literature is central to his work, now that the forces of narrow cultural nationalism, which denounced Borges in the 1940s and 1950s, have become weakened, perhaps terminally.

In short, there is no writer in Argentine literature more Argentine than Borges. In his work this national cultural tone is not expressed in the representation of things, but rather in his exploration of how great literature can be written in a culturally marginal nation. Borges's work always deals with this issue, one of the most important questions for a relatively young nation, without strong cultural traditions, located in the extreme south of the former Spanish dominions of Latin America; the extreme south, too, of the most culturally impoverished Viceroyalty of Spain – one which had no great Precolumbian indigenous cultures of its own.

There are many reasons for seeing Borges as a universal cosmopolitan writer. He *is* that of course, and his work lends itself to such a reading. One can read Borges without reference to *Martin Fierro*, to Sarmiento or to Lugones. Such a reading would explore his great philosophical pre-occupations, his tense but permanent relationship with English litera-ture, his system of quotations, his erudition drawn from the minutiae of encyclopaedias, his work as a writer on the body of European literature and on what this literature has constructed as the 'Orient'. It would explore his cluster of symbols, mirrors, labyrinths, doubles, or his predilection for Nordic mythology and the cabbala. But a reading constrained within these limits would not pick up the tension that runs through Borges's work, that almost imperceptible movement which destabilizes the great traditions once they intersect with a River Plate dimension (in the sense that roads cross – but also in the sense that races mix).

Borges wrote at this meeting of roads. His work is not smooth, nor is it located precisely on a homogeneous cultural base. Rather, there is a tension in it caused by mixing with, and feeling a nostalgia for, a European culture which can never wholly offer an alternative cultural base. At the heart of Borges's work there lies a conflict, and this book will attempt to read his work as a response to that conflict rather than seeing it as elegantly unproblematical writing. I have sought to highlight this tension which, in my opinion, runs through Borges's work and defines it: a game on the edge of various cultures, which touch on the borders, in a space that Borges would call *las orillas*. In this way, a writer emerges who has two sides, who is at once cosmopolitan and national.

Borges the cosmopolitan (educated in Switzerland during the First World War and earlier raised with the English books of his father's library) returned to Argentina in the early 1920s, there to remain until a very few years before his death. He at once began posing basic questions. How was it possible to write literature in Argentina, a marginal country with an immigrant population, living in a port city, Buenos Aires? This town was in the process of becoming a metropolis, but it was still very much surrounded by the countryside — that immensity of nature from which the echoes of a rural criollo* culture could still be heard, even as modernization was eliminating it: above all as myth. Facing his criollo past, Borges asked how it was possible to avoid the pitfalls of local colour, which can only produce a regionalist and narrowly localist literature, without relinquishing that density of culture which comes from the past and is part of our own history. This question presupposes another, concerning literary tradition. Still very close to Borges stood the nineteenth-century gauchesque literature of the River Plate, the writings of Sarmiento, the almost family saga of the civil wars that preceded the organization of the nation state, the battles between Indians and whites throughout implacable, bloody and unjust decades. These traces of the Argentine past never disappeared from Borges's work. Rather, one of his goals was to gather up the scattered fragments of that tradition and to rearticulate within his own writing the writing of other Argentines who had now disappeared.

The first thing Borges does is to reconstitute a cultural tradition for that eccentric place that is his country. This aesthetic and ideological intent can be seen in his work from the 1920s until the publication in

---

*Throughout this book the word 'criollo' refers to a population and culture with Hispanic, colonial or nineteenth-century origins. Criollos are the descendants of Spaniards, and may eventually have acquired a few drops of Indian blood. The adjective and the noun 'criollo' refer to landowners and rural workers and gauchos. The rural culture of the nineteenth century, its system of production, customs, codes and values is also referred to as criollo. But the term is also used to describe colonial urban formations. In the first decades of the twentieth century, 'criollo' was used to mark a strong distinction from foreigners of immigrant origin.

1935 of *Historia universal de la infamia* (*A Universal History of Infamy*), a collection in which he published his first story about *compadritos* (hard men) and knife fighters. But his task does not end there: the problem of Argentina culture recurs in Borges's fictions right up to his last books, in particular in the stories of *El informe de Brodie* (*Dr. Brodie's Report*), which were published in the mid-sixties. Borges reinvents a cultural past and reconstitutes an Argentine literary tradition at the same time as he is reading foreign literatures. Furthermore, he is able to read foreign literatures in the way that he does precisely because he is reading, or has read, Argentine literature. In Borges's cosmopolitanism is a condition that allows him to invent a strategy for Argentine literature. Conversely, the reordering of national cultural traditions enables Borges to cut, select and reorder foreign literatures without preconceptions, asserting the right of those who are marginal to make free use of all cultures. By reinventing a national tradition, Borges also offers Argentine culture an oblique reading of Western literatures. From the edge of the West, Borges achieves a literature that is related to foreign literature but not in any subordinate way.

Herein lies Borges's originality: as a writer–critic, a short story writer–philosopher, he obliquely discusses in his texts the major topics of contemporary literary theory. This has turned him into a cult writer for literary critics who discover in him the Platonic forms of their concerns: the theory of intertextuality, the limits of the referential illusion, the relationship between knowledge and language, the dilemmas of representation and of narration. The Borges literary machine fictionalizes these questions, producing a *mise en forme* of theoretical and philosophical problems without ever allowing the development of the tale to lose completely the brilliance of ironic distance or the careful and anti-authoritarian position of agnosticism. Against all forms of fanaticism, Borges's work offers the ideal of tolerance. This feature has not always been identified with sufficient emphasis, perhaps because we left-wing Latin American intellectuals have been too slow to recognize it in fictions which deal with questions about order in the world. The fantastic themes of Borges, which critics have universally commented upon, offer an allegorical architecture for philosophical and ideological concerns. If the defence of the autonomy of art and of formal procedures is one of the pillars of Borges's poetics, the other, more conflictual, pillar is the philosophical and moral problem of the fate of human beings and the forms of their relation to society. These concerns, which coexist with metaphysical preoccupations about the organization of the real in a cosmos, are highlighted throughout the following pages.

It has been my intention not to decide on one reading of Borges (which is of course a rather arrogant aspiration), but to offer different ways of reading him that take into account the invariably dual and conflictual nature of his literary work. I do not want to establish a version of Borges that opts for the 'cosmopolitan' writer at the expense of the 'Argentine' writer, or to choose between the writer of fantastic fictions and the writer haunted by philosophical questions. The originality of Borges — one of the many forms of his originality — lies in his resistance to being found where we are looking for him. Something of the old avant-garde writer remains in this resistance to replying to what is being asked or of asking himself what it is that one wants to hear from him.

If Borges's literature has one very particular and undeniable quality, it must be sought in the conflict that disturbs the strict organization of his arguments and the perfect surface of his writing. Placed on the limits between cultures, between literary genres, between languages, Borges is the writer of the *orillas*, a marginal in the centre, a cosmopolitan on the edge. He is someone who entrusts literary processes and formal procedures with the power to explore the never-ending philosophical and moral question of our lives. He is someone who constructs his originality through quotations, copies and the rewritings of other texts, because from the outset he conceives of writing as reading, and from the outset distrusts any possibility of literary representation of reality. These pages have attempted to be faithful to all these tensions in their rereading of Borges today, at a time when his work seems to be shrouded by the fame that accompanied his final years, and by the immovable spectre of a posthumous glory.

Acknowledgements

In Cambridge I enjoyed the warm and intellectually vigorous support of my colleagues at the Centre for Latin American Studies and the generous academic and material hospitality of King's College. These institutions, and the friendships that they brought, offered optimum conditions for pursuing this work. James Dunkerley and in particular Donald Nicholson-Smith suggested numerous ways for correcting my original English texts. I am also grateful for the generosity of an old friend of mine and of my country, John King, who had the idea for this book.

PART ONE

WRITING ON THE EDGE

ONE

A Landscape for Borges

Buenos Aires in the 1920s and 1930s. Every attempt at periodization is controversial, but these decades undoubtedly witnessed spectacular change. At issue is not just the aesthetic avant-gardes and economic modernization, but modernity as a cultural style permeating the fabric of a society that offered little resistance, either politically or socially. The socioeconomic processes set in train in the second half of the nineteenth century altered not only the urban landscape and ecology of the city, but also the lived experiences of its inhabitants. Thus Buenos Aires is interesting both as a physical space and as a cultural myth. The city and modernity presuppose one another because the city was the stage for the changes wrought by modernity: it exhibited them in an ostensible and sometimes brutal fashion, disseminating and generalizing them.

It is not surprising therefore that modernity, modernization and the city should merge the programmes, values and categories that allow us to describe new physical spaces, and material and ideological processes. Inasmuch as Buenos Aires was altered, before the eyes of its inhabitants, with a speed attuned to the rhythm of the new technologies of production and transport, the city may be perceived as a symbolic and material condensation of change. As such it is both celebrated and judged. A stage on which we pursue the phantoms of modernity, the city is the most powerful symbolic machine of the modern world.

The idea of Buenos Aires cannot be seen as separate either from the changes caused by modernization or from the fulfilment of other ideas belonging to the nineteenth-century institutional projects of Domingo F.

Sarmiento and Juan Bautista Alberdi. The city had defeated the rural world; immigration from Europe and internal migrations (which became significant from the mid thirties) offered a new demographic base. Economic progress superimposed its model on reality, the more so because the Depression did not affect Argentine development for an extended period. The illusion prevailed that the peripheral nature of this South American nation could now be seen as a fluke of its history and not as a feature of its present.

At the same time, the idea of Argentina as peripheral, as a tributary cultural area — a notion that appears inadequate or even monstrous when compared with a European model — persisted in a contradictory yet not inexplicable fashion.[1] Opposing sentiments — celebration, nostalgia or criticism — are scattered through the cultural debates about the city. In the twenties and thirties, moreover, some vigorously political myths were constructed around Buenos Aires. The metaphor of the port-city, for example, as a voracious centripetal machine emptying the rest of the country, which could not yet consider itself urban even though urbanization was spreading rapidly.[2] In these years the desire for and the fear of, the city came to occupy a central space in Argentine society and culture.

The desire for the city is as strong in the Argentine nineteenth-century tradition as the rural utopias. In this sense, the intellectuals of the twentieth century adhere to the paradigm of Sarmiento rather than to that of José Hernández, author of *Martín Fierro* and champion of the rights of the gaucho. The only exception to this are Ricardo Güiraldes, a cosmopolitan ruralist if this oxymoron may be permitted, and Borges who invented images of both Buenos Aires and of the Argentine rural past.

The ideal space of the city was apprehended not only in political terms, as in various chapters of Sarmiento's famous works *Facundo* or *Argirópolis*, not only as a theatre where the intellectuals discovered the defining mix of Argentine culture, but also as an imaginary realm which literature could invent and inhabit. The city informed historical debates, social utopias, dreams beyond reach, landscapes of art. To touch the city was to reach a territory that had sustained many of our inventions. But, perhaps most important, the city was the stage par excellence for the intellectual, and both the writers and their public were urban actors.[3]

Buenos Aires had grown in a spectacular fashion in the first two decades of the twentieth century. As Walter Benjamin has argued, the modern city makes the *flâneur* socially possible, and credible in a literary sense. The *flâneur* can observe these changes with the anonymous gaze of one who will not be recognized since society is no longer the space of immediate relationships, but has become a space in which relationships are mediated through institutions and through the market. In his journey from the suburbs to the centre, the *flâneur* crosses a city which has been defined in broad terms, but which still contains many plots of land which have not yet been built upon, wasteland and *calles sin vereda de enfrente* (streets without the sidewalk on the other side), in Borges's felicitous phrase. But by the early thirties the cables of electric wire had replaced the old systems of gas and kerosene. The sky of Buenos Aires was already criss-crossed by telephone wires and the roofs were full of radio aerials, for radio came to Buenos Aires as early as it did to the United States. Motorized transport, in particular the trams and the trains, had expanded and diversified. The inhabitants of the city lived at an unprecedented pace: the experience of speed, the experience of artificial light — and of long-distance communications, which would soon give rise to a powerful culture industry — provided a new set of images and perceptions. Those who, like Borges, were older than twenty in 1925 could remember with nostalgia the city at the turn of the century, and could confirm the difference.

Technology provided the new machinery for the urban stage; it offered new definitions of space and time: futurist utopias linked to the speed of transport, to the electric light which produced a profound break with the rhythms of nature, and to the great enclosed precincts which were another kind of street, of market-place and of meeting-place.

This new type of aesthetic-ideological formation is shown, in the first place, in the mingling of discourses and practices: the modern city is always heterogeneous precisely because it is defined as a public space. The street is a place, among others, where different social groups wage a war of symbolism. Architecture, urbanism and painting reject the past, correct the present and imagine a new city. The painter Xul Solar,[4] companion of the avant-garde groups of the twenties and someone often quoted by Borges, deconstructed plastic figurative space, making it at once abstract and technological, geometric, inhabited by the symbols of a specific magical-scientific fiction. The aviators drawn by Xul float in planes where flags and insignia mix: here is an extremely elaborate image which in a sense summarizes the technical modernization and national diversity of Buenos Aires.

Architectural utopias are also a complex response to the process of transformation. Between 1927 and 1935, Wladimiro Acosta imagined an architectural fiction, the 'city block' as an alternative to the truly chaotic growth of Buenos Aires. From another point of view, the intellectual aristocrat Victoria Ocampo became a patroness and Maecenas of architectural modernism and promoted it through her magazine, *Sur*,[5] which first began publication in 1931. Modernism, for Ocampo, could be seen as an instrument for the purification of taste, indispensable in a city where immigration had left material traces, where diverse national origins had produced stylistic anarchy. Modernism would propose a programme of homogenization in face of the stylistic *volapuk* (heterogeneity) of immigrant origin: its volumes and facades would discipline the street.

The impact of these transformations, which took place in a relatively short period of time, had a subjective dimension: in reality men and women could remember a city that was different to the one in which they were now living. And, furthermore, that earlier city was again different to that of their childhood or adolescence. These people's past underlined what had been lost (or what had been gained) in the modern city of the present.

Buenos Aires had become a cosmopolitan city in terms of its population. What scandalized or terrified the nationalists in 1910, the centenary of Argentine independence, also influenced the intellectuals of 1920 or 1930: the European immigrants who had begun to arrive in the last third of the nineteenth century, now totalled tens of thousands. Even in 1936 foreigners accounted for 36.1 per cent of the total population of the big cities of the Littoral provinces. From a global perspective they were younger and their women bore more children than Hispanic-criollo women, so that immigrants and sons of immigrants accounted for 75 per cent of total population growth in Argentina. These were sectors that became literate and had access to compulsory primary schooling. They began the hard journey of moving up in society and many of them joined the ranks of intellectuals and journalists.

The space of the great modern city (a model to which Buenos Aires approximated in the twenties and to which it came even closer in the thirties) is an arena for national and cultural mixture where, hypothetically, all meetings and borrowings are possible. What we find here, therefore, is a culture defined by the principle of heterogeneity which, in the urban space, makes differences extremely visible. In the city, the

boundaries between private and public are constructed and reconstructed incessantly; there the social sphere creates the conditions for
mixture and produces the illusion, or the effective possibility, of dizzying
rises and falls. And if the quick road to fortune makes the city the site for
a utopia of upward mobility, the possibility for anonymity converts it,
into the preferred, indeed the only possible, place for the *flâneur*, for the
conspirator (who lives his solitude in the midst of other men), for the
erotic voyeur who is electrified by the gaze of the unknown woman who
passes by. Vice and the breaking of established moral codes are
celebrated as the glory or the stigma of the city. Public space loses its
sacredness; everyone invades it, everyone considers the street as a
common place, where offers are multiplied and at the same time
differentiated, where wares are displayed, creating desires which no
longer recognize the limitations imposed by hierarchy.

But there exists another street, a symbolic space which frequently
appears in almost every Argentine writer of the twenties and thirties,
from Oliverio Girondo to Raúl González Tuñón, via Roberto Arlt and
Borges.[6] In the street, time is perceived both as history and as the present.
This street is certainly proof of change but it may also become the site
where these changes are turned into a literary myth. For the modern
street, criss-crossed by electric cables and the rails of the street-cars,
could be denied, as writers looked behind it for the remains of a street
which might not yet have been touched by modernization – that
imaginary corner of the suburb invented by Borges in the image of *las
orillas*, an indeterminate place between the city and the countryside. On
the one hand there is the fascination with the downtown street where
aristocrats are as much in evidence as prostitutes, where the newspaper
vendor slips the envelope with cocaine to his clients, where journalists
and poets frequent the same bars and restaurants as criminals and
Bohemians. On the other hand, there is the nostalgia for the neighbourhood street, where the city resists the stigmas of modernity, although the
neighbourhood itself may have been a product of urban modernization.

Yet the heterogeneity of this public space – accentuated in the
Argentine case by the new cultural and social mixtures provoked by
pressing demographic change – put different levels of literary production in contact with each other, establishing an extremely fluid system of
aesthetic circulation and borrowing. There was already a vigorous and
well-defined middle-brow public, stratified socially, ideologically and
politically. By the mid 1930s the rate of illiteracy in Buenos Aires was

only 6.64 per cent. Here, then, was a social space occupied by a vast potential reading public which included many of the lower social sectors. Mass circulation books, serial novels and magazines were produced for this new public, covering a range of tastes from literature 'for pleasure and consolation' to explicit didactic and social propaganda. Successful publishing houses like Claridad undertook print-runs of between ten and twenty-five thousand copies, publishing a little bit of everything: European fiction, philosophical and political essays, popular science, poetry. These cheap books filled the shelves of the poor reader. They offered a literature that was morally responsible, pedagogically useful and accessible both intellectually and economically. This type of publishing house built up a reading public which, thanks also to a new type of journalism, was forever changing and expanding. Two large newspapers, *Crítica* and *El Mundo*, began publication in 1913 and 1928 respectively. The distinguishing features of this new journalism for middle- and lower-class sectors were a new rhythm, brief articles, unusual news items, crime reports, sport and cinema, sections dedicated especially to women, to daily life, to children; cartoons and a great emphasis on graphic material. But these newspapers also offered employment to writers new to the intellectual field and even to those of patrician origin, such as Borges, who ran the colour supplement of *Crítica* for a short period. The new journalism and the new literature had many points of contact and were together responsible for the establishment of a modern form of professional writer as well as for consolidating the reading preferences of the new public. Here was a culture that was becoming more democratic in production, distribution and consumption.

A reformist and eclectic Left also established institutions for the dissemination of culture — popular libraries, lecture halls, publishing houses, magazines — aimed at those sectors which remained on the margins of 'high' culture. The questions of internationalism and social reform were posed in terms of a process of education for labouring masses gradually becoming incorporated into a democratic and secular culture. In literary terms, this meant offering a series of translations principally from Russian and French realism) and a poetics of humanitarianism.

The magazines in the style of *Caras y Caretas* (which first appeared towards the end of the previous century) were modernized, articulating discourses and information of a different sort and tending to present an integrated symbolic world in which cinema, literature, popular music, articles on daily life, fashion and comic strips all had a place. The sentimental *feuilletons* and the magazines mapped out a horizon of desire, offered models for pleasure, and worked for and on a public just beginning to consume literature. Partly through this medium, and partly under the powerful spell of silent films, this public could now dream the modern dreams of cinema, fashion, cosmopolitan comfort, the universe of the large department stores, shopping displays, fashionable restaurants, and dance halls. This news-stand literature was based on pleasure, the pleasure of eroticism, of sentimentalism and of daydreaming. Those who produced this culture also intermixed, contributing both to the expansion of the system and to its instability: cultural borrowings and influences, and texts that oscillated between 'high' and 'low' culture, were all offered to a public of great cultural diversity.

But this very heterogeneity was disturbing. The large modern newspapers, the magazines, radio, cinema, variety shows and theatre, precisely because they addressed different publics, tended to turn a cultural spotlight on the social differences between old criollos, immigrants and sons of immigrants. The juxtaposition of these different groups aroused nationalisms and xenophobia, and reinforced a feeling of nostalgia for the city as it had been before 1920.

Buenos Aires could now be viewed with a retrospective gaze which put into focus a past more imaginary than real (as is the case with the early Borges), or it could be discovered in the emergence of a working-class and popular culture, formed under the influence of cinema and radio and organized by a rapidly developing cultural industry. Capitalism had profoundly changed the urban space and made the cultural system more complex. This complexity began to be lived not only as a disturbing issue but also as an aesthetic theme, rife with the conflict of programmes and poetic theories which fuelled the battles of modernity. Humanitarian realism took up arms against the avant-garde, but discourses with different functions also clashed: journalism against fiction, politics versus the general essay, the written word as against the cinematographic image.

The debates concerning the establishment of a cultural canon spanned the literary magazines. The old criollos were not ready to admit that a literary language might also be produced by writers whose parents had not been born in Argentina, whose accent gave them away as immigrants from the suburbs and outskirts of the city. The cultural and ideological complexity of the period is the product of these different influences, and of the mixture of different discourses from Cubist painting or avant-garde poetry to tango, cinema, modern music or the jazz-band.

The heterogeneity of discourses, from advertising to journalism, from poetry to *Trivialliteratur*, from radio soap operas to cinema melodrama forced literature itself out of its isolation, as it found itself obliged to incorporate these diverse influences. Roberto Arlt is a case in point. The link between his novels and the *feuilleton* have been discussed at length by critics. Yet Arlt shows his relationship not just to 'elite' literature but also to the new texts and practices of science, chemistry, physics, and of those simulacra of popular science which then circulated in Buenos Aires as hypnotism, mesmerism, telepathic transmission and the like. Arlt's writing, or the desires of his characters, cannot be understood if no reference is made to this 'lore of the poor', picked up in cheap manuals, in the popular libraries which operated in all the neighbourhoods, in the workshops of harebrained inventors who had experienced the blinding illumination of electricity, the fusion of metals, galvanism and magnetism.

On the other hand, Arlt's futuristic vision of the city could not have existed without the impact of new ways of representing the 'theatre' of the city — especially films. The Buenos Aires he depicts has something of the nightmarish quality of the city portrayed in the German expressionist films then being shown in Buenos Aires. Arlt visits the city as no one before him. He goes to the prisons and hospitals, he criticizes the sexual habits of lower middle-class women and the institution of marriage, he denounces the selfishness of the petty bourgeoisie and the ambition which corrupts the rising middle-sectors, he stigmatizes the stupidity which he uncovers in the bourgeois family.

Arlt's practice of mixing and transforming different elements can be placed in a more general perspective: the formation of the writer by non-traditional modes, including, pivotally, journalism and different versions of popular culture. Both influences originated in the new industrial culture and presupposed the emergence of non-traditional publics, and hence new ways of reading and establishing genres.

The new urban landscape, the modernization of the means of communication, the impact of these processes on customs and habits, offered a framework and a series of challenges for intellectuals. In the course of a very few years, intellectuals had to process in their own lived experience changes which affected traditional relationships, forms of producing and disseminating culture, styles of behaviour, ways in which the literary canon was established and the organization of institutions. Social conflicts cast their shadow over cultural and aesthetic debates. The questions of language (who speaks and writes an 'acceptable' Spanish untainted by foreign influences introduced by the immigrants), of cosmopolitanism (what is a legitimate internationalism and what is a perversion of the nation?) and of *criollismo* (which forms can be incorporated into a new aestheticand which are merely picturesque and folkloric deviations?) are some of the topics included in the debate. At the same time, there is always an assessment of the past couched in nostalgic or in critical terms.

In Europe the process of modernity is characterized by a position of relative independence with respect to the past, a position which Carl Schorske describes as a growing indifference: the past is no longer seen in terms of functional continuity. Schorske refers to a 'death of history', as a necessary precondition for the establishment of modernity as a global discourse and as a hegemonic practice in the literary and cultural spheres: the victory of Nietzsche.[7] But in the case of Borges and many of the Argentine avant-garde writers there is a clear attempt to give the past a new function. The severity of the break with cultural traditions is related to the force that these traditions exert. The break will be more radical in a society where modern forms of intellectual relations are already firmly rooted, where aesthetic and ideological fractions and parties have been formed, and where there are clear disputes over the canon, over symbols and authorities. When faced with a strong, consolidated tradition, confrontation appears as a necessary strategy from the point of view of new artists and new poetics. In Argentine culture this general relationship with the past is given a specific form by the reading and imaginary recuperation of a culture much affected by immigration and urbanization.

Furthermore, in Argentina as in other Latin American countries there is a difference between the forms of artistic modernity, which stress autonomy, and the forms of the avant-garde break, which seek a public stage for the airing of artistic conflicts. The process of cultural modernization, carried out in the twentieth century, is centrally concerned with the programmes of humanism and the Left. For the avant-garde 'the new' offers the basis for establishing aesthetic value, whilst for the intellectuals of the Left this basis must be found in reform, in revolution or in some other kind of transformational utopia. In this context modernity is located in processes of change in the bases of cultural practice.

Political, aesthetic and cultural ideologies thus confronted one another in a debate which had Buenos Aires as its stage and, frequently, as its protagonist. The modern city is a privileged space where the concrete and symbolic forms of a culture in the process of transformation are organized in the dense network of a stratified society. These social differences were represented or distorted in the intellectual field and were present in both institutional and aesthetic conflicts. Intellectuals felt that the battles being waged in the cultural field were important chapters in a process in which, somehow, the future was at stake. They produced different reactions to this heterogeneity; some defended a spiritual elite which might purify or, at least, denounce the artificial and corrupt nature of Argentine society. Others resorted to myths and images of the past which might serve to restructure current relationships, a tactic that often led to the invention of a past. Still others recognized the diversity of the present and hoped by means of that diversity to construct a culture.

Affected by change, immersed in a city which was no longer that of their infancy, obliged to recognize the presence of men and women who, by being different, destroyed any notions of an original unity, and considering themselves to be different to the literary elites of Spanish-criollo origin, the intellectuals of Buenos Aires attempted, in a figurative or a direct manner, to respond to the main questions of the day. How to accept or to obliterate the differences in lived experience, in values and in practices? How to construct a hegemony for the process in which they all participated, amidst the conflicts and uncertainties of a society in transformation? The answers to these questions of the twenties and thirties remained relevant until at least the 1950s. This was a period of uncertainties, but also of great certainties, of rereadings of the past and of utopias in which the representations of the future and of history collided in texts and polemics. The culture of Buenos Aires was driven forward by 'the new', although many intellectuals also lamented the irreparable nature of change. Modernity is a stage for restorative fantasies but also for loss, which brings with it feelings of nostalgia.

Notes

1. The discourse of the essay in the thirties and forties would have as one of its main themes this notion of 'monstrosity', which emerged from modernization and which, for its authors, would not have been a necessary companion to modernity in Europe. In *Radiografía de la fampa* (1933) Ezequiel Martínez Estrada sets out his criticisms of a nation which has not responded to the promises and dreams of its 'founding fathers'. Massive immigration had left Argentina with only a degraded image of Europe (an image anticipated by the conception of the Spanish conquest conceived of as a rape); Buenos Aires was a mask which merely succeeded in showing in a too-evident way the failure of civilization in America. Less pessimistic, Eduardo Mallea's *Historia de una pasión argentina* (1937) evinces astonishment at the great city but, at the same time, imagines that the visible and material city covers another invisible reality on whose values Argentinian culture should be founded.

2. Raúl Scalabrini Ortiz, in the 1930s, began his task of denouncing the economic destruction of Argentina by British imperialism which, in laying out the railway network, was alleged to have deformed the national territory and to have converted Buenos Aires into the area whither all riches produced by the provinces unjustly flowed. The works of Scalabrini Ortiz had a powerful impact on the constitution of nationalist ideologies and myths which, decades later, would come together in Peronism.

3. For José Luis Romero this productivity of the urban (and of the urban elites) is one of the main features of the cultural and institutional tradition of Latin America. See *Latinoamérica; las ciudades y las ideas*, Mexico City 1976.

4. See Aldo Pellegrini, Prologue, *Xul Solar 1887-1953*, Paris 1977.

5. See John King, *Sur: A Study of the Argentina Literary Journal and its Role in the Development of a Culture, 1931-1970*, Cambridge 1986.

6. Oliverio Girondo, *Veinte poemas para ser leídos en el tranvía*, in *Obras Completas*, Buenos Aires 1990; Raúl González Tuñón, *El violín del diablo*, Buenos Aires 1926, and *Miércoles de ceniza*, Buenos Aires 1928; Jorge Luis Borges, *Poemas (1922-1943)*, Buenos Aires 1943; Roberto Arlt, *El juguete rabioso, Los siete locos, Los lanzallamas*, and *El amor brujo*, in *Obras completas*, Buenos Aires 1981.

7. See Carl Schorske, 'The Idea of the City in European Thought: Voltaire to Spengler', in Oscar Handlin and John Burchard, eds., *The Historian and the City*, Cambridge (Mass.) 1963.

TWO

Borges and Argentine
Literature

Borges's work offers one of the paradigms — perhaps *the* paradigm — of Argentine literature. This is a literature constructed, like the nation itself, in a marginal country, out of different influences: European culture, the criollo tradition and the Spanish language spoken with a River Plate accent. The place which Borges inhabits, which he invented in his first three books of poetry published in the nineteen twenties,[1] is what he called *las orillas*. From the outset, Borges rejected the kind of utopian ruralism that Ricardo Güiraldes had put forward in *Don Segundo Sombra* (1926), a classic novel which traces the education of a boy in the customs and morals of the pampas, guided by the most successful figure of a gaucho mentor. For Borges, the imaginary landscape of Argentine literature should instead be an ambiguous region where the end of the countryside and the outline of the city became blurred.

Borges worked with all the meanings of the term *orillas* (edge, shore, margin, limit) to create a powerful ideologeme that would define his early poetry and prove powerful enough to reappear in many of his short stories. By means of this ideologeme Borges created a myth for the city, which in his opinion stood sorely in need of myths:

> There are no legends in this land and not a single ghost walks through our streets. That is our disgrace. Our lived reality is grandiose yet the life of our imagination is paltry ... Buenos Aires is now more than a city, it is a country, and we must find the poetry, the music, the painting, the religion and the metaphysics appropriate to its greatness. That is the size of my hope and I invite you all to become gods to work for its fulfilment.[2]

In those years in Buenos Aires, the term *orillas* described the poor suburban neighbourhoods that lay in close proximity to the pampas that surrounded the city. The *orillero* was the inhabitant of those neighbourhoods, usually considered coarse and often violent, who preserved many of the customs and attitudes of his recent rural past. The *orillero* worked in semi-rural and semi-urban enterprises such as the slaughterhouses, where many of the skills of the rural workhand were needed and employed. He knew how to use a knife, like his forefather the gaucho, and he continued, so the legend goes, to use it as a weapon in duels. A more mythic version of the *orillero* was the *compadrito*, a character who became well known later through tango lyrics. The archetypal *orillero* belongs to the criollo cultural tradition, prior to the arrival of Italian and other European immigrants. But, as Borges himself ironically admitted, the sons of the Italian immigrants who managed to become integrated into criollo culture could also aspire to being *compadritos*. However, by the time Borges began to write, *orilleros* and *compadritos* were losing their more aggressive and distinctive traits and blending into a common popular culture. When he evokes the *orillas*, Borges is writing more about the last decades of the nineteenth century and the first decades of this century than about the twenties and thirties. Aware of this temporal displacement, he uses the past tense and inserts dates that point to something that has been lost, and can no longer be retrieved:

> Calle Serrano,
> you are no longer the same as at the time of the Centenario
> then you were more sky and now you are pure buildings[3]

For Borges, the *orillas* possess the qualities of an imaginary territory, an indeterminate space between the plains and the first houses of the city, an urban-criollo topology, defined in the now classic formulation as the street *sin vereda de enfrente* (without a sidewalk on the other side). The frontier between city and countryside widens on the *orillas* when these become a literary space. At the same time this frontier becomes porous. The landscape of the *orillas* is punctuated by vacant stretches of wasteland and mud walls with niches, by the clarity of the decorative grilles and the hedges of cina-cina and honeysuckle, by patios which break up the indeterminacy of the sky:

> Patio, channelling the sky,

the patio is the slope
down which the sky pours into the house[4]

The *carros del verano* (summer carriages) come to the *orillas* and they smell of the plains. The pale pink, sky-blue and whitewashed walls of the rural houses are also the colours of the *orillas*. In the *orillas*, imperceptibly, the *pulpería*, the rural drugstore and saloon, becomes an *almacén* (grocery store), and the intersection of two rural roads becomes a street corner.

From a memory of Buenos Aires which is almost not his own, Borges sets against the modern city this aesthetic city without a centre, built totally on the matrix of a margin. What was evident to his contemporaries becomes invisible in Borges's poetry of the 1920s. Two of his most eminent contemporaries, the novelist Arlt and the poet Girondo were fascinated by the movement of the new: trains and tramways, high buildings, the city blocks. Borges, by contrast, reconstructs something which probably had never quite existed and which, for that very reason, could be transformed into nostalgia. The threatened *orillas* of literature can be found in any part of the city, precisely because they are margins with no centre. They can be defined in the movement of the *flâneur* who wanders with no fixed aim through the far-flung suburbs and the more familiar petty-bourgeois neighbourhoods, drinking in the past that unfolds before his eyes in the buildings and the landscape:

There was a time when this neighbourhood was a friendship,
an argument of aversions and affections, like other things of love;
that faith yet barely persists
in some distant feats which will die:
in the milonga that calls to mind the Five Corners,
in the patio like a firm rose beneath the climbing walls,
in the unpainted sign that says, still, The Flower of the North,
in the men playing guitars and cards in the general store,
in the static memory of the blind man.
This dispersed love is our disheartened secret.
Something invisible is disappearing from the world,
a love no wider than a tune.
The neighbourhood is leaving us,
the stout little marble balconies do not bring us face to face, with the sky.[5]

In one of his many prologues to *Martín Fierro*, the major work of nineteenth-century Argentine literature, Borges affirms that 'One function of art is to bequeath an illusory yesterday to men's memory.'[6] This illusory yesterday is also, or perhaps fundamentally, a place which Borges reclaims from the countryside, because he prefers 'those long streets which overflow the horizon, where the suburb becomes steadily poorer and tears itself apart outside in the afternoon.'[7]

Borges liberated *las orillas* from the social stigma of the *compadrito*, who was also occasionally called an *orillero*. Instead of considering the *orillas* as a frontier from which it is only possible to leap into the rural world of *Don Segundo Sombra*, Borges pauses there and makes the border a territory and a metaphor. He chose to locate a literature on that margin, recognizing that in some way a coded form of Argentina could be found there. This might explain his reluctance to acknowledge the gaucho revival heralded by Ricardo Güiraldes in *Don Segundo Sombra*, and his weakness for a minor poet of Buenos Aires, Evaristo Carriego, on whom Borges wrote a book-length essay, published in 1931.

Borges could not help but be interested in Carriego. There, perhaps in a clumsy fashion, could be found a subject-matter which the elite writers of the period considered marginal. In the first decade of this century, the centre of the field was occupied by Leopoldo Lugones and by *modernismo*, a poetry rich in sound and rhyme, in exotic images built on an elaborate system of visual, tactile and musical perceptions, and inspired by French Parnassianism and Symbolism, by Victor Hugo and Walt Whitman. Although *modernismo* (and its major poet Rubén Darío) had been highly original in its capacity to combine different aesthetic influences and blend them into a distinctive new tone and cultural landscape, by the twenties it had exhausted its potential, and its novelty had faded to become part of what could be considered the literary mainstream. The avant-garde writers opposed, and showed contempt for, the mainstream: *modernismo* had become a well-established movement that had to be overthrown.

Borges was extremely hostile to *modernismo* and to Lugones and his own poetry would be completely different to their practices. And, if *modernismo* was the centre of the literary system, Borges considered that Carriego was precisely on the margin: a writer who had tried to be a *modernista*, only to find subsequently, in a dozen poems on the suburbs, a mild form of sentimentalism which prefigured the nostalgic tangos of Homero Manzi.

Simply by opposing Carriego to Lugones, all the aesthetic-ideological

23

hierarchies which had previously organized Argentine literature could be turned on their heads. The elimination of Lugones was one of the tasks to which Borges, with great conviction, applied his critical irony, beginning with his first texts of the 1920s. *Evaristo Carriego* is a fundamental chapter in this literary activism. In Carriego Borges also recognized a pre-text, in the most literal sense of the term. Carriego is the text prior to Borges's own texts; he wrote something that Borges was never to write, but something that Borges needed as a position from which to work out a theory of Argentine literature. Carriego's *La canción del barrio* (The Song of the Neighbourhood) is a secret ur-text, a necessary hypothesis for Borges's early poetry.

Borges's biography of Carriego is, of course, also a pre-text in other ways.[8] In a prologue added some twenty-five years later, Borges reveals one of the motives underlying this book. He wanted to know, in a biographical and literary sense, what stood outside the family house of his childhood in the neighbourhood of Palermo:

> What lay, meanwhile, on the other side of the iron railings? What vernacular and violent fates were being acted out a few paces from me, in the smoky bar or in the dangerous wasteland? What was that Palermo like, or how beautiful would it have been if it had been like that?[9]

The history of Palermo, which makes up the first chapter of the book, is a pretext for history, in which some of the images of the *orillas* and the *compadritos*, which Borges had already worked on, are interwoven with details whose only function is poetic. The second chapter, 'Una vida de Evaristo Carriego' (A Life of Evaristo Carriego), begins by offering the paradox 'that an individual wishes to awake in another individual memories which had only ever belonged to a third': it begins, in other words, by critically questioning the very idea of biography. Thus an exclusively subjective logic binds together the 'facts' of Carriego's life with those which Borges attributed to him and which turn into Borges's memories. The next two chapters (supposedly on 'Misas herejes' [Heretical Masses] and 'La canción del barrio' (The Song of the Neighbourhood), two sets of poems by Carriego) abound in open and hidden references to the cultural myths of the suburbs and give weight to Borges's assertion that Carriego should be read as a poet of the *orillas*. So *Evaristo Carriego* mimics a biography but in reality it is written as a chapter of a mythical history of Buenos Aires and, at the same time, as a literary manifesto, albeit ironic and understated. Borges never abandoned this book and over the course of three decades he continued at leisure to add supplementary pages, prefaces, quotations in English, mini-narratives, letters — all related to their subject-matter in a very oblique manner.

This biography is also the work of a timid man, as Borges described himself some years later, when he published *A Universal History of Infamy*. The character 'Borges' who writes this book is as much an invention as Carriego, and the imaginary topology of the suburb, the limit between the city of the upper and the middle classes and the city of the *compadrito* is drawn as one of the spaces of Borges's own literature. Rather than a biography, which clearly it is not, *Evaristo Carriego* is a pre-text and a treatise: the first volume of an encyclopaedia of that suburban Tlön which Borges invents under the guise of Buenos Aires. And in this volume, as in the encyclopaedia of Tlön, a conception of art would of course find a place. Borges would later comment rather severely on the mythical and literary construction of the *orillas* and the *compadritos*. In the Afterword to *Doctor Brodie's Report* he condemns the elaborate fantasy of his very typical *porteño** short story 'Streetcorner Man' — an 'all too famous extravaganza', writes Borges. Yet the poems written in the twenties, this story, and *Evaristo Carriego* were necessary moments in the development of his writing, and although he rejects the baroque profusion of *cuchilleros* in his early work, Borges never altogether distanced himself from the ideologeme that he constructed in the twenties, which had the originality of being deeply Argentine without falling into the deadly trap of either conventional literary nationalism or of literary realism.

> If one seeks to deny the autonomous existence of visible and palpable things, one might easily reach this conclusion by thinking: reality is like that image of ourselves that comes out of every mirror, a simulacrum that exists because of us, comes with us, waves and then leaves, but which can always be found if we go looking for it.[10]

This idealist profession of faith, written by Borges when he was little over twenty years old, rests on a metaphor that stresses the notion of the simulacrum. Literature, in particular, invents those spaces whose power

---

Porteño is an adjective which refers to those born or brought up in Buenos Aires, the port city, and by extension the positive and negative qualities of the city's inhabitants.

of persuasion lies in the illusion produced by and in the text (forcing what Borges likes to call, quoting Coleridge, 'the willing suspension of disbelief'). 'Carriego' and the *orillas* are not in this sense simulacra of a lesser poet or of Buenos Aires, but rather of what Borges writes and, above all, of the place whence he writes. The reality of that character and that space is founded, precisely, on invention.

In this way, Borges lays the foundations of his literature by opposing two dominant concepts. It has often been said, and I have aimed to show here, that Borges's first books, his articles in the avant-garde journals *Proa* and *Martín Fierro* (see Chapters 7 and 8), signify a break with Lugones and with *modernismo*. They answer the question of how to write after and in opposition to Lugones. It seems to me that this point is sufficiently clear and, therefore, I would prefer to move on to another one: I believe that Borges is also proposing a literature that is different to Güiraldes's rural novel *Don Segundo Sombra*.

It is true that he never subjected Güiraldes to the games of literary terrorism that he played on Lugones. Güiraldes was on his side in the avant-garde movements of the 1920s, he directed *Proa* with Borges, and Güiraldes often acknowledged, in one of his fulsome articles, that Borges was among those young writers who had a mission to reform and renew Argentine literature. Nonetheless, it is arguable that Borges saw himself as very distant indeed from the aesthetic principles underlying *Don Segundo Sombra*. Güiraldes's *gauchismo* would have been, for Borges, excessively compact. Weighed down by rural minutiae, full of descriptions of gaucho tasks, respectful in his attitude to *costumbrismo*, Güiraldes must have been a problematic novelist for Borges.

In 'The Argentine Writer and Tradition', Borges offers a form of defence of *Don Segundo* which, after a careful reading, awakens our suspicions:

> The nationalists tell us that *Don Segundo Sombra* is the model of a national book; but if we compare it with the works of the gauchesque tradition, the first thing we note are differences. *Don Segundo Sombra* abounds in metaphors of a kind having nothing to do with country speech but a great deal to do with the metaphors of the then current literary circles of Montmartre. As for the fable, the story, it is easy to find in it the influence of Kipling's *Kim*, whose action is set in India and which was, in turn, written under the influence of Mark Twain's *Huckleberry Finn*, the epic of the Mississippi. When I make this observation, I do not wish to lessen the value of *Don Segundo Sombra*; on the contrary, I want to emphasize the fact that, in order that we

might have this book, it was necessary for Güiraldes to recall the poetic tech-
nique of the French circles of his time and the work of Kipling which he had
read many years before; in other words, Kipling and Mark Twain and the
metaphors of French poets were necessary for this Argentine book, for this
book which, I repeat, is no less Argentine for having accepted such influences.[11]

This somewhat overstated defence of *Don Segundo* is impeccable, but,
precisely for that reason, I would like to examine this statement in the
context of the whole article. A few paragraphs earlier Borges had put
forward his celebrated and well-known assertion, 'd'après Gibbon',
concerning the absence of camels in the *Koran*, an absence which was
justified since Mohammed was sure of his own Arab identity. The
absence of camels, reasoned Borges, exaggerating his argument into a
paradox, should be sufficient to prove the Arabness of the *Koran*. The
example allows him to express his desire for an Argentine literature
discreet in its use of local colour. Without pausing, he goes on to criticize
his first books ('forgettable and forgotten') which overflowed with *compadritos*, mud walls and seedy suburbs. Immediately afterwards comes
the defence of *Don Segundo* quoted above.

It is not difficult to conceive of this as a contradiction, but I would
prefer to consider it as a further argument, containing a great deal of
sophistry, in Borges's polemic with literary nationalism. Borges takes a
text which for nationalists represents the 'essence' of Argentina, and
shows that it is in fact shot through with many cross-cultural references.
The irony of the phrase 'contemporary cliques of Montmartre', to which
Borges was not attached, is just one of the many clues which lead us to
believe that, rather than offering a defence of *Don Segundo*, Borges takes
the novel, as well, as a pre-text, using it in a polemical argument about
nationalism. He praises it, but the arguments which precede and follow
that praise tend considerably to weaken his praise.

For Borges *Don Segundo Sombra* was too obviously a criollo novel. The
abundance of local references detracted from, rather than proved, its
'Argentine nature', for they were used to excess. The frequency and self-
sufficiency with which Güiraldes presented *gaucho* lore, experiences and
learning went against what Borges considered the basic Argentine qualities: reticence and constraint were absent from the stylistic and narrative
display. There are too many horses in *Don Segundo Sombra* for its pretensions as a national text to be taken seriously.

Borges prepares the path for the rest of his argument, and skilfully leads it to its ideological-aesthetic conclusion, by abandoning the Güiraldes novel and stating the issue in a direct and general way:

> What is our Argentine tradition? I believe we can answer this question easily and that there is no problem here. I believe our tradition is all of Western culture, and I also believe we have a right to this tradition, greater than that which the inhabitants of one or another Western nation might have. I recall here an essay of Thorstein Veblen, the North American sociologist, on the pre-eminence of Jews in Western culture. He asks if this pre-eminence allows us to conjecture about the innate superiority of the Jews, and answers in the negative; he says that they are outstanding in Western culture because they act within that culture and, at the same time, do not feel tied to it by any special devotion.[12]

The same, Borges adds, applies to the Irish and to Argentines and South Americans in general: 'We can handle all European themes, handle them without superstition.' The fabric of Argentine literature is woven with the threads of all cultures; our marginal situation can be the source of our true originality. It is not based on local colour (which binds the imagination to empiricist control) but on the open acceptance of influences.

This is precisely what Borges achieves in his first book of stories, *A Universal History of Infamy*, working with second-hand materials, European versions of Oriental fictions, lives of North American bandits and gunmen, almost insignificant episodes concerning Chinese pirates, false Persian prophets or Japanese warlords. Published in 1935, *A Universal History of Infamy* followed the book on Carriego; it included a dozen short stories which Borges would describe years later as the 'exercises of a man who was timid'. (Too timid, perhaps, to write his own stories, so that he used plots from various sources to compose them — yet bold enough to publish a most atypical and original collection). Within Western culture and its versions of the Orient, Borges goes in search of marginal stories which are alien to the great literary tradition and which, in some cases, reveal his taste for the detective genre or his devotion to adventure novels. His sources are minor or little-known books (except for Mark Twain's *Life on the Mississippi*) which he reworks with the freedom of a marginal who knows he is writing in the margins.

He chooses themes so clearly exotic that whether or not they are exotic vis-à-vis River Plate culture is an almost meaningless question.

And furthermore, these themes undergo a process of verbal creolization which in a deliberate way anticipates the last story in the book, and Borges's first tale of *compadres*, 'Streetcorner Man' (itself a rewriting of 'Hombres pelearon' [Men Fought], an extremely brief text he had published years before in *Martín Fierro*).

Distance, Borges would argue, if it is conceived of as a geographical, cultural and poetic displacement, and assumed as a Latin American right, not only makes fiction possible, but also creates the conditions for the reader's pleasure. *Don Segundo Sombra* is once again the butt of Borges's irony in the short story 'The Gospel according to Mark', written several decades later in 1970. Here Borges gives fictional form to the same theoretical proposition. On a ranch in the township of Junín, in the pampas, towards the end of the twenties, a man from Buenos Aires is cut off by a flood with the Gutres, a family of rural workers:

> In the whole house, there was apparently no other reading matter than a set of the *Farm Journal*, a hand-book of veterinary medicine, a deluxe edition of the Uruguayan epic *Tabaré*, a *History of Shorthorn Cattle in Argentina*, a number of erotic or detective stories, and a recent novel called *Don Segundo Sombra*. Espinosa, trying in some way to bridge the inevitable after-dinner gap, read a couple of chapters of this novel to the Gutres, none of whom could read or write. Unfortunately, the foreman had been a cattle drover, and the doings of the hero, another cattle drover, failed to whet his interest. He said that the work was light, that drovers always travelled with a pack-horse that carried everything they needed, and that, had he not been a drover, he would never have seen such far-flung places as the Laguna de Gómez, the town of Bragado, and the spread of the Núñez family in Chacabuco.[13]

What Borges achieves with this reading of *Don Segundo* to the peons is, ultimately, to reaffirm the freedom or, rather, the necessity of cultural mixture. The Gutres gain no pleasure from Güiraldes's novel, because they can perceive that here is no difference between it and their own rural world. The Gospel which Espinosa reads to them afterwards, on the contrary, fascinates them with a story which is at once full of miracles and the exotic. And as a consequence, behaving as tragically active readers, they re-enact that text on the *estancia* by crucifying the man who told it to them. The Gutres's emotions are therefore stirred not by similarity but by difference. This sinister parable of the power of reading demonstrates that, for Borges, cross-cultural blending is one of the imaginative strategies needed to liberate literary invention from the claims of realism and the repetitive routine of everyday experience.

'Funes the Memorious' can be understood as a fictional mise-en-scène of the enslavement of a discourse by direct experience. Funes has an infinite memory but is incapable, Borges asserts, of thinking: 'To think is to forget differences, generalize, make abstractions. In the teeming world of Funes, there were only details, almost immediate in their presence.'[14] Literature is, precisely (and specifically), a symbolic practice that breaks with the immediacy of memory, perception and repetition. Literature works with the heterogeneous, it cuts, pastes, skips over things, mixes: operations which Funes cannot carry out with his perceptions, nor, as a result, with his memories. For Borges, real memory is related in the main to oblivion.

Irineo Funes, an inhabitant, like Borges, of 'a poor South American suburb', is doomed to remain in thrall to the material of his experience. Enclosed within a world where there are no categories merely perceptions, Funes must attempt impossible tasks — among them the art of classification, so often the object of Borges's irony, as in 'The Analytic Language of John Wilkins'. Funes, in fact, invents a system of words designed to replace the infinite series of numbers, so revealing both the mysterious force of his memory and the futility of the task:

> He told me that in 1886 he had invented an original system of numbering and that in a very few days he had gone beyond the twenty-four-thousand mark. He had not written it down, since anything he thought of once would never be lost to him. His first stimulus was, I think, his discomfort at the fact that the famous thirty-three gauchos of Uruguayan history should require two signs and two words, in place of a single word and a single sign. He then applied this absurd principle to the other numbers. In place of seven thousand thirteen, he would say (for example) *Máximo Pérez*; in place of seven thousand fourteen, *The Railroad*; other numbers were *Luis Melián Lafinur, Olimar, sulphur, the reins, the whale, the gas, the cauldron, Napoleon, Agustín de Vedia*. In place of five hundred, he would say *nine*. Each word had a particular sign, a kind of mark; the last in the series were very complicated. I tried to explain to him that this rhapsody of incoherent terms was precisely the opposite of a system of numbers [...] Funes did not understand me or refused to understand me.[15]

Borges deploys his irony on two levels. On the one hand, there is a very obvious reference to the system of words-instead-of-numbers used by gamblers and bookies in clandestine lotteries and other betting games — which places Funes's invention in the most trivial cultural context. On the other hand he reveals the difficulties of translating from one code into another. Funes is attempting to translate, and expresses the conviction that systems are perfect analogies of what they stand for. Borges claims exactly the opposite: to translate always means to lose, to misplace, to divert, and if this is not understood we fall into the trap of a naive belief in the ultimate identity of languages. In the face of semiotic systems and reality, a false hope can arise that representation and straightforward communication are possible.

A *conte philosophique* on literary theory, 'Funes the Memorious' can be understood as a parable dealing with the possibilities and impossibilities of representation, because Funes experiences to the limit the problems of translating perception, experience, and memories of experience into discourse. Funes is enthralled by what Borges would have called the disordered chance of realistic representation, and his situation is desperate: the duration of what is narrated (the told) and the duration of the narration (the telling) coincide in his discourse in a perfect fashion: 'Two or three times, he had reconstructed a whole day; he had never hesitated, but each reconstruction had required a whole day.' Funes ignores ellipsis and cannot sever the continuum of remembered time in order to organize it into the artfully crafted development of the narrative; he is not free to forget and, hence, he is not able to choose. Thus he is condemned to repetition, and his discourse, though fascinating as a philosophical monstrosity, can never aspire to the originality achieved by the freedom to choose and to reject. Funes is not a paradox but a hyperbolic image of the devastating effects of an absolute and naive realism which trusts the 'natural' force of perceptions and events. He ignores the process of the construction of reality, and is thus incapable of constructing a discourse that could free him from his enslavement to absolute mimesis. If for Funes time were infinite (as it is for God), his memory would no longer frustrate his endeavours. But literature, like any narrative, rests upon the unavoidable principle that time offers a limit to the representation of what takes place in time.

Without doubt, Borges is dealing with the problem of how to write in general, and not only of how to write in Argentina. Yet both questions seem to come together in the theoretical fiction 'Pierre Menard, Author of the *Quixote*'. In this story, irony and paradox generate ambivalence, which is in any case Borges's preferred mode of address. The text criticizes the very 'knowledge' it produces. After completing a long list of written exercises which relate, albeit in an overtly ridiculous way, to translation, paraphrase and pastiche, Menard had undertaken the task of rewriting, word by word, Cervantes's novel:

> He did not want to compose another *Quixote* – which is easy – but the *Quixote itself.* Needless to say, he never contemplated a mechanical transcription of the original; he did not propose to copy it. His admirable intention was to produce a few pages which would coincide – word for word and line for line – with those of Miguel de Cervantes.[16]

Borges states that the chapters of *Don Quixote* which Menard was able to write before his death 'are more subtle' than those of Cervantes, although, at the same time, they are identical. What is the meaning of this paradox? It becomes clear that the attribution to Menard of these chapters of *Don Quixote* enriches the text of Cervantes through displacement and anachronism. The idea of the fixed identity of a text is destroyed, as are the ideas of authorship and of original writing. With Menard's method, original writings do not exist and intellectual property is called into question. Meaning is constructed in a frontier space where reading and interpretation confront the text and its (always ambiguous) relationship to any claim to literal meaning and objectivity. In fact Borges is using the paradox of Menard to assert that all texts are the rewriting of other texts (in an endless interplay of textuality and meaning) – but that, *at the same time,* all texts are read against a cultural background which forms the fleeting course of meaning into a historical pattern:

> Let us examine Chapter XXXVIII of the first part, 'which deals with the curious discourse of Don Quixote on "arms and letters"'. It is well known that Don Quixote (like Quevedo in an analogous and later passage in *La hora de todos*) decided the debate against letters and in favour of arms. Cervantes was a former soldier: his verdict is understandable. But that Pierre Menard's Don Quixote – a contemporary of *La trahison des clercs* and Bertrand Russell – should fall prey to such nebulous sophistries! ...
>
> It is a revelation to compare Menard's *Don Quixote* with Cervantes'. The latter, for example, wrote (part one, chapter nine): '... truth, whose mother is history, rival of time, depository of deeds, witness of the past, exemplar and adviser to the present, and the future's counsellor'. Written in the seven-

teenth century, written by the 'lay genius' Cervantes, this enumeration is mere rhetorical praise of history. Menard, on the other hand, writes: '... truth, whose mother is history, rival of time, depository of deeds, witness of the past, exemplar and adviser to the present, and the future's counsellor'. History, the *mother* of truth: the idea is astounding. Menard, a contemporary of William James, does not define history as an inquiry into reality but as its origin. Historical truth, for him, is not what has happened; it is what we judge to have happened. The final phrases — *exemplar and adviser to the present, and the future's counsellor* — are brazenly pragmatic.[17]

The process of enunciation modifies any statement. As a study of linguistics in the twentieth century has emphasized, this principle destroys and at the same time guarantees originality as a paradoxical value which is related to the 'enunciation': it comes from the activity of writing and reading, not tied to words but to words in a context. As an ultimate consequence of this hypothesis, Borges lays claim to the productivity of reading and demonstrates the impossibility of repetition; although every text presents the variation of a few topics, it also reveals the radical difference between them. There is no way, Menard says or Borges says, that a text can be the same as its double or as its exact transcription. All texts are, from this point of view, absolutely original, which amounts to saying that none can aspire to this special quality. Borges is fascinated by translations (which are another mode of transcription, more arduous, perhaps, and ultimately impossible). In his comments on the Homeric versions, he had already discovered that 'to presuppose that every recombination of elements is necessarily inferior to its original, is to presuppose that working-copy 9 is necessarily inferior to working-copy H — as there can only be working-copies. The concept of the *definitive text* corresponds only to religion or to fatigue.'[18]

Literature is composed of versions. The paradox of Pierre Menard illustrates the process of writing, by taking it to the limits of the absurd and of impossibility, yet at the same time making it visible. This proposition, formed in the geographical-cultural margin of the River Plate, offers a new situation for the writer and for Argentine literature, whose operations of mixture, of free choice without 'devotions' (to use Borges's term), do not have to respect the hierarchical order attributed to originals. If no originality is attached to the text, but only to the writing or reading of a text, the inferiority of the margins vanishes and the peripheral writer is entitled to the same claims as his or her European predecessors or contemporaries.

Notes

1. *Cuaderno San Martín, Luna de enfrente* and *Fervor de Buenos Aires.*
2. Jorge Luis Borges, *El tamaño de mi esperanza*, Buenos Aires 1926, pp. 8–9.
3. 'A la calle Serrano', in *Indice de la nueva poesía americana.*
4. 'Un patio', in *Fervor de Buenos Aires*, Buenos Aires 1923.
5. 'Barrio Norte', from *Cuaderno San Martín*, in J.L. Borges, *Poemas (1922–1943)*, Buenos Aires 1943.
6. J.L. Borges, *Prólogos con un prólogo de prólogos*, Buenos Aires 1975, p. 94. The text quoted was written in 1962.
7. *Inquisiciones*, Buenos Aires 1925, p. 58.
8. 'The innocent biography proves to be a turbulent, insidious text', writes Sylvia Molloy, *Las letras de Borges*, Buenos Aires 1979, p. 27.
9. *Evaristo Carriego*, Buenos Aires 1965, p. 11.
10. *Inquisiciones*, p. 119.
11. 'The Argentine Writer and Tradition', *Labryrinths*, London 1970, p. 216.
12. *Labyrinths*, p. 218. On the basis of this same quotation, Sylvia Molloy develops the concept of Borges's 'lateralness' in Western culture.
13. 'The Gospel According to Mark', in *Doctor Brodie's Report*, London 1976, p. 18.
14. 'Funes the Memorious', in *Labyrinths*, p. 94.
15. 'Funes the Memorious', *Labyrinths*, pp. 92–93.
16. 'Pierre Menard, Author of the *Quixote*', *Labyrinths*, pp. 65–6.
17. *Labyrinths*, pp. 68–9.
18. 'Las versiones homéricas', in *Discusión, Obras completas*, Buenos Aires 1975, p. 239.

THREE

Tradition and Conflicts

Nostalgia can only be felt for something which has been lost, in fact or in the imagination. In a Buenos Aires transformed by the processes of urban modernization, where the criollo city was obliged to take refuge in a few neighbourhood streets, and even there underwent changes that affected both its physical and its demographic profile, Borges invented a past. He worked with elements that he discovered in (or ascribed to) the Argentine culture of the nineteenth century, a culture that for him had a solidity to be found not so much in books as in a sort of family tradition. Yet even these fragments, found in the fading images and deeds of his criollo ancestors, were threatened by time, modernity and oblivion:

> My ancestors struck up a friendship
> with these distances
> conquering the prairie's closeness....
> As a town-dweller, I no longer know these things.
> I come from a city, a neighbourhood, a street.[1]

As an Argentine, Borges was part of an endangered tradition. No matter how tenuous the presence of this tradition might be, he felt that he belonged to it as much as it belonged to him. But like his ancestors the Spaniards, who forged a friendship with the pampas, Borges had lost a 'natural' link with Europe. Although he was educated in Geneva and was a friend, in Madrid, of the ultraist writers he met when he was very young, although he repeatedly points out that the first novels he read as a child — even *Don Quixote*, which he read in translation — were in English, Borges could not but feel the problem of a culture which was defined as European but which was not altogether so, because it was developed in a peripheral country and blended with the criollo world. If he could enter and leave two cultures at will, this freedom had its cost: there was something artificial and distant in his relationship to both. This is the freedom of Latin Americans, Borges would have answered, which is upheld by the awareness of something missing. To read all world literature in Buenos Aires, to rewrite some of its texts, is an experience which cannot be compared to that of the writer who works on the secure terrain of a homeland that offers him or her an untroubled cultural tradition. Although it could be argued that this is very seldom the case with great twentieth-century European writers, those outside the European tradition consider that native Europeans have a close affinity with their 'natural' cultures. Yet the fact that they are embedded in a culture that is, for them, inevitable, deprives them of the very freedom that Latin Americans can deploy. Freedom is our fate.

Borges dramatized the limits and conflicts of this freedom in several fictions that are very similar in their differences: 'The South', 'The End' and 'Story of the Warrior and the Captive'. Let us see how these fictions reveal some of the key topics of Borges's literature.

'The End' deals with the meaning and the place of Argentine culture and attempts to answer the following question: what are the elements that make up Argentine literature, and how is Argentine literature related to world literature? It is also revealing about Borges's sense of possessing a literary and a cultural past: the ways in which he modifies a heritage.

The Argentine avant-garde of the twenties and thirties, to which Borges belonged, had to offset the influence of some very important writers, notably Leopoldo Lugones, who occupied the centre of the literary system. Lugones was not only the most important *modernista*, the national peer of Darío, but also a most visible and influential intellectual. As poet laureate, he represented what the literary avant-gardes, and Borges himself, loathed: rich rhymes, sumptuous images, highly wrought exoticism, decadent eroticism. As a public figure, he solemnly asserted his pre-eminence and made ample use of his supreme power to pass judgement on the value of contemporary literature. He published in the prestigious newspaper *La Nación*. His most disparate opinions on many different topics were taken as trustworthy and the social and intellectual elite, including the President of the Republic and his ministers, flocked to his lectures, which were major events in Buenos Aires intellectual life.

In 1916, Lugones had given a very influential interpretation of the nineteenth-century gauchesque poem by José Hernández, *Martín Fierro*, which he read as a national epic.[2] The central character in the poem, the gaucho Martín Fierro, was for Lugones a symbol of Argentine qualities and values. This myth gained its strength from the very fact that gauchos, as members of a free, poor, rural population not wholly incorporated into the labour market but coerced into it according to the needs of a very primitive exploitation of the pampas, or else drafted into the army to defend the frontier from Indian raids, were no longer to be found on the plains. They had disappeared, to be replaced by rural wage-earners who worked in the *estancias*, mastered the traditional skills with the knife, the lasso and the horse of their fathers and forefathers, but had none of the gaucho's rebelliousness.

Martín Fierro (published in two parts, in 1872 and 1880) was presented by Lugones as an allegory of the Argentine past and a symbol of an Argentine essence. It was a timely invention, for immigrants from Italy, as well as Germany and Central Europe, were arriving by the thousands in Buenos Aires, and the intellectuals were worrying about the future of their culture and what some of them took to calling the 'Argentine race', by which they meant the elite and that portion of the working-class population whose origins could be traced back to the colonial period. The gauchesque poem *Martín Fierro* used to be learnt by heart, and was taught in schools along with the official version of local history according to which the gauchos had willingly given their lives in the Wars of Independence against Spain only to be rewarded with social instability, as the nation-state extended its control over all the territory of the Argentine, liquidating regional resistance and waging genocidal campaigns against the Indians. The poem provided the basis of a mythical reorganization of our nineteenth-century history and a no less mythical model of nationality. The themes and many of the stanzas of *Martín Fierro* were quoted frequently, not only by members of the criollo population but also by immigrants who took the gaucho as a symbol of the nationality they were trying to understand and assimilate into.

The criollo elite, to which Borges belonged, considered that *Martín Fierro* was a poem that should be placed at the mythical origins of Argentine culture and, at the same time, that it was a canonical text. The gauchos as such had disappeared, but their virtues were blended into the Argentine character and could be presented as a paradigm and a guide for the ideological and cultural integration of immigrants. In fact, the gaucho Martín Fierro was not just a man full of virtues. In José Hernández's poem, he had been abused by the police, had lost his family and his few properties and become an outlaw. He had fought the Indians after his compulsory recruitment into the frontier army, where he had found more misery and injustice. He had deserted and fled into Indian territory in order to avoid the consequence of this crime and of other acts, not all of them honourable. He had killed without evident reason, provoked duels without obvious motive and insulted people out of bravado or drunkenness, as in the episode with the black gaucho whose brother he finally meets in the story by Borges. All in all, Martín Fierro was a complex figure, a victim of an unjust system as well as an untamed rural knife-fighter. Curiously enough, the criollo elite managed to turn him into the epitome of the national character (overlooking his unruly nature), while anarchists of immigrant origin turned him into a model and inspiration for social revolt. Thus anyone writing in Argentina in the first four decades of this century had to examine and grapple with the gaucho myth, whether in order to reject it, to rework it or to adopt it. Both the avant-garde and the anarchists had used the name of Martín Fierro as a title for two very important journals: the cultural supplement of an anarchist paper, at the beginning of the century, and a literary magazine, published in the mid twenties by young poets and writers, among them Borges (see Chapter 7). Fierro was a cultural heritage about which almost everyone in the intellectual and political field had something to say. The meaning of the poem was the object of many debates and conflicts in the formation of cultural hegemony, and when the avant-garde reinterpreted the poem they entered into an aesthetic and ideological discussion with the canonical reading put forward by their literary enemy Lugones.

Borges was no exception. He wrote dozens of essays on *Martín Fierro* and gauchesque literature, prologues and introductions to many editions of *Martín Fierro*, and a small book on the poem in the mid fifties. *Martín Fierro* is one of his literary obsessions, and as late as the sixties we find him declaring in *El hacedor* that the battles of the civil wars and of the Wars of Independence might be forgotten, that Perón himself would someday be forgotten, but that Hernández had dreamt of a duel between two gauchos that would indefinitely repeat itself: 'the visible armies have gone away and only a poor duel remains; this dream of one man is part of everybody's memories.'³

In opposition to Lugones's view of *Martín Fierro* as a national epic, Borges points out that it has many novelistic elements. Epic heroes, states Borges, need to be perfect; Martín Fierro is morally imperfect, and through that imperfection belongs to the tradition of characters in novels. In creating this character Hernández had brought the gauchesque tradition to a close, because his poem was the most perfect of the cycle and after it only second-rate gauchesque literature could be written. But he had also left to future writers a book that could be read and reread, commented on and rewritten like (in Borges's comparison) the Bible and Homer.

On the one hand, then, *Martín Fierro* had to be considered an essential text of Argentinian literature. Borges considered Lugones's own interpretation deeply futile and unfortunate: comparing the gaucho with Homeric characters was one of his most pretentious and foolish ideas. The poem had to be freed from the dead weight of Lugones's epic and hyperbolic criticism and re-installed in a tradition that could prove productive to current literature. In fact the poem had to be read against the grain, and set free from the straitjacket of previous interpretations.

Borges achieved this in two ways: through his essays on *Martín Fierro* and other poems of the gaucho cycle, and through some very important fictional texts. Here we shall consider this second strategy, what Borges did with *Martín Fierro* in his own short stories. Although traces can be found in many stories, I have selected one, 'The End' because it seems to me at once to close the gaucho cycle and to recognize its importance in the national literature — something Borges, however, as also the most cosmopolitan of Argentinian writers, would never have done explicitly.

In 'The End', written in 1944, Borges depicts the death, in a duel, of Martín Fierro. In the last Canto of Hernández's poem, Fierro parts from his children after hearing their life stories (they had been separated for twenty years, during which time all the family had suffered). They now split up once more because, as Fierro says, the tragic life of the gaucho prevents him from establishing a home and living with his family. He is an outlaw, because he has killed a man, a Moreno, without reason; he is an outlaw because he deserted from the army while he was serving on the frontier against the Indians. Although Fierro has repented of his crimes (for which he holds society partly responsible), he knows he has no chance of living peacefully within the rural criollo world. Accepting this nomad destiny, he rides away, promising not to reappear and to be silent for ever after. But, before parting, he states that all faults committed should be paid for, in a famous line: No hay plazo que no se cumpla/ni deuda que no se pague' ('No debt should be left unpaid/all accounts arrive sooner or later').

In Hernández's poem, Martín Fierro has slain a gaucho of black origin, the Moreno, at the entrance of a *pulpería* without any reason, out of sheer impulse and racial prejudice. Later on, a brother of this Moreno has challenged him to sing in order to discover which of the two was better at improvising topical subjects with a guitar. In this contest (which the gauchos called a *payada*) Fierro is again the winner. But he has a moral debt to pay and the brother of the Moreno has the right to expect Fierro to come back and submit himself to the customary code of revenge for an unlawful death. Fierro knows this and does not try to escape his destiny. Nevertheless, this second meeting between Fierro and the brother of his victim never takes place in the poem.

Borges imagined the story from this point on, that is to say, he imagined what Hernández never wrote, and wrote it himself. Seven years have elapsed since the day Fierro sang the *payada* with the Moreno's brother. Fierro is by now almost an old man, waiting for death with no hopes save one: that he should have a decent death. According to his honour code, a decent death, in the case of a man who has moral debts to pay, can be found in a duel. The Moreno shares this belief: although he did not fight Fierro the last time he had seen him, because he was reluctant to stage a duel in front of Fierro's children, he is patient enough to wait for a second opportunity. He knows he is going to meet Fierro again, he knows that Fierro will come to him in order to pay his debt, to compensate for the crime committed when Fierro killed the Moreno's brother.

Borges's story begins with the Moreno alone in a *pulpería* (rural store) waiting for Fierro: he knows that Fierro is going to honour that tacit appointment. Fierro, for his part, has no wish to escape, because the inevitable duel that will follow is as good a way as any other to put an end to his life. He knows that every debt should be paid one way or another, and a duel is an archaic ceremony that he respects: it is embedded in his culture and in his sense of honour. 'Destiny has made me kill and now, once more, it has put a knife in my hand', says Fierro to the Moreno when, at last, he reaches the *pulpería*. Both men engage in a dialogue where honour and destiny are the main topics: 'I was sure, señor, that I could count on you', says the Moreno. 'And me on you', replies Fierro. 'I made you wait many days, but here I am.' The Moreno recalls their last meeting, seven years before, when Fierro did not accept the duel because his children were present. 'I told them, among other things, that one man should not shed another man's blood.' The Moreno replies: 'You did well. That way they won't be like us.'[4]

And this is almost everything that happens: both characters recall their past, the past that was told by Hernández in his poem of 1872 and 1880. Borges is writing an end to it — and an end to the gauchesque cycle. Thus he incorporates this cycle into his literature and draws a final portrait of Fierro as an old man who is going to die. Very different from the portrait drawn by Lugones of the gaucho as national epic hero, Borges's Fierro is a sober man who respects his destiny and knows that nothing can be done to alter it. But far from being a national paradigm, he is a defeated man who can only wait for a decent death. From a moral point of view, this end corresponds to a rural culture, where fatalism is a sort of popular philosophy; and where retaliation is a right. In this sense Borges captures the ideological dimension of Hernández's poem and liberates it from the epic interpretation of Lugones and similar writers. Fierro is not a hero, but a man profoundly embedded in the primitive culture of the plains. In fact, by accepting his destiny, Fierro becomes a character of Borges's fictions.

From another point of view, let us call it allegorical, Borges is doing what neither Lugones nor Hernández did: he is putting an end to the cycle, as if arguing that *Martín Fierro* has to be rewritten, adding Fierro's death to the open end of Hernandez's poem before it can become, once again, a productive source of Argentine literature. But this rewriting also means, allegorically, the end of Fierro as a character and as a symbol: Fierro pays his debts with his own death and, above all, Fierro is defeated by someone (a Moreno, a man of another race, considered inferior to the criollo breed) who could not defeat him in Hernández's poem.

These intertextual relations between poem and story are a clue to Borges's literature and to his position with regard to Argentina's historical and cultural past. Once again in a meditation on *Martín Fierro* (in a short piece where he retells the life story of one of the poem's principal characters, the soldier and later outlaw Tadeo Isidoro Cruz) he clearly states that *Martín Fierro* is 'a notable book; that is to say a book whose matter may be "all things to all men", for it is capable of almost inexhaustible repetitions, versions and perversions'.[5]

Versions and perversions: that is exactly Borges's rereading of literary tradition. First, there was Evaristo Carriego, a minor popular poet whom Borges turned into a kind of prefiguration of his own literature; then there were the minor stories he retold in *A Universal History of Infamy*; and finally there is his rewriting of *Martín Fierro*, in which he adopts what he says is the only attitude a man can have towards tradition: betrayal. The mode of this betrayal is to contradict other interpretations of the text, and to go back to Hernández himself, leaping over the pretentious reading of the poem as an epic. In so doing he develops in 'The End' one of his most enduring themes: that a man should comply with his fate, which reproduces *en abîme* the destiny that others have endured.

But by presenting Martín Fierro's death in a duel, Borges also kills the most famous literary character in Argentine culture. He closes the poem that Hernández had left open: the death of Martín Fierro is both the death of a character and the end of a literary cycle. In this way, Borges answers an ideological and aesthetic question: what should an avant-garde writer do with tradition? The insertion of his short story 'The End' into the gauchesque cycle is an original way of dealing with the question. Borges does not reject the literary past in toto; on the contrary, he faces up to the most important text (the sacred text) and weaves his own fiction with some of the threads Hernández had left loose in his poem. Thus is the story of Martín Fierro re-enacted, and at the same time modified for ever.

I will now consider 'The South' and 'Story of the Warrior and the Captive', taking them together because, in a sense, they can be read as different versions of the same theme. Juan Dahlmann, the main character in 'The South', is, like Borges himself, the product of cross-cultural mixing. It is well known that Borges's grandmother was an Englishwoman married into a criollo family, to a man who, around 1870, commanded a military settlement on the border of Indian territory. It is also well known that Borges, on many occasions, told his readers that he grew up in a very typical Buenos Aires neighbourhood, Palermo (where Evaristo Carriego had also lived), and that he remembers hearing the music of guitars and seeing *compadritos* or knife-men who were mythically brave, outlaws or bodyguards of conservative politicians — maybe both at the same time. He tells us about the old house of his childhood, separated from the street by the iron gate of colonial architecture, and, in the middle of that quite conventional criollo setting, an immense library of English books where he read for the first time *The Arabian Nights* (in Burton's translation), Stevenson, Mark Twain, and *Don Quixote* in an English version which he liked much more than the Spanish original. We know that his first literary work, when he was nine or ten, was the translation of a story by Oscar Wilde which was published in a newspaper in Buenos Aires and which was so perfect that everybody thought it had been done by Borges's father.

Like his English grandmother, who had lived in a humble village in the midst of the pampas, surrounded by Indian territory, Borges feels that he belongs in these two very different worlds: the criollo space of his military grandfather, and the English (and, all in all, European) tradition of his grandmother. He would later crystallize this myth of divided origin in the short story entitled 'Story of the Warrior and the Captive', where an Englishwoman, Borges's grandmother, discovers that another English-woman who had been abducted and held captive by the Indians, preferred, when offered the choice, to return to the Indian village where her heart, and more than her heart, had been captivated by the brutality of a new life. The Englishwoman is fascinated and at the same time horrified by this adoption of a different, and in all respects alien, culture or, as Borges's parents and Borges himself would put it, by this process of becoming a barbarian:

> Perhaps the two women felt for an instant as sisters; they were far from their beloved island and in an incredible country. My grandmother uttered some kind of question; the other woman replied with difficulty, searching for words and repeating them, as if astonished by their ancient flavour. For some fifteen years she had not spoken her native language and it was not easy for her to recover it. She said she was from Yorkshire, that her parents had emigrated to Buenos Aires, that she had lost them in an Indian raid, that she had been carried off by the Indians and was now the wife of a chieftain, to whom she had already given two sons, and that he was very brave. All this she said in a rustic English, interwoven with Araucanian or Pampan, and behind her story one could glimpse a savage life: the horsehide shelters, the fires made of dry manure, the feasts of scorched meat or raw entrails, the stealthy departures at dawn, the attacks on corrals, the yelling and the pillaging, the wars, the sweeping charges on the haciendas by naked horsemen, the polygamy, the stench and the superstition. An Englishwoman had lowered herself to this barbarism. Moved by pity and shock, my grand-mother urged her not to return. She swore to protect her, to retrieve her children. The woman answered that she was happy and returned that night to the desert.[6]

Borges clearly thinks that crossing a cultural border and living on the edge of a frontier (what he calls in his poetry the *orillas*, the borderline) is a pattern not only of the captive's story but of his own, and metonymically of Argentine literature. The English captive could be described by an oxymoron: a fair, blue-eyed, Indian woman. At the beginning of the 'Story of the Warrior and the Captive', Borges quotes Benedetto Croce, who had in turn quoted a Latin historian on the subject of Droctulft, the Lombard warrior who, 'during the siege of Ravenna, left his companions and died defending the city he had previously attacked'.[7] Borges confesses to having for years been intrigued by — and indeed strangely sympathetic to — Droctulft's decision. It was only when he came to link this story to that of his English grandmother that he was able to grasp the meaning that underlay the use of the singular 'story' (not 'stories') in the title of his own text. Droctulft was not a traitor, says Borges, but a convert:

> The wars bring him to Ravenna and there he sees something he has never seen before, or has not seen fully. He sees the day and the cypresses and the marble. He sees a whole whose multiplicity is not that of disorder; he sees a city, an organism composed of statues, temples, gardens, rooms, amphitheatres, vases, columns, regular and open spaces. None of these fabrications (I know) impresses him as beautiful; he is touched by them as we now would be by a complex mechanism whose purpose we could not fathom but in whose design an immortal intelligence might be divined.[8]

The fair blue-eyed captive was also a convert, although the meaning of her adoption of Indian culture could seem to us (but not to an 'immortal intelligence') to be the opposite of that of Droctulft. Both the warrior and the captive chose to abandon their world enthralled by an otherness that they did not understand.

Borges uses the same theme in his story 'The South'. Juan Dahlmann, the protagonist of the story, is like Borges the descendant of mixed ancestors. His grandfather Johannes Dahlmann was a Protestant priest of German origin and his mother's father, Francisco Flores, was a military man and a criollo of Spanish origin who had fought against the Indians. Dahlmann — like Borges in the forties when this story was written — is an obscure librarian with vague criollo sympathies who has kept up, albeit with some economic difficulties, the country house of an estancia inherited in the south of Buenos Aires province. Like Borges too, Dahlmann cherishes old books and rare editions. One evening, on arriving home with a volume of the *Arabian Nights,* he is wounded in the head by an open window which he bumps into unawares as he is climbing the stairs to his house. The wound on his forehead is deep and dangerous. It becomes infected, and Dahlmann goes down with a fever. After many days of unconsciousness and delirium, the doctors declare him to be out of danger. Weak and confused, he decides to spend some time in his estancia, which he has not visited for years.

At this point the story is given a twist. 'Reality', writes Borges, 'favours symmetries and slight anachronisms.'[9] The story of Dahlmann's illness turns into the story of his impossible recovery, because his decision to go south, into the plains, will be shown to be much more dangerous than the physical wound that is already almost healed.

Dahlmann takes a train and carries with him the volume of the *Arabian Nights* he had been reading on the evening of his accident. Lulled by the movement of the train, the monotony of the landscape and the childish delight produced by the trip, he keeps repeating to himself that the next day he will be in the estancia, in the middle of the pampas, in the deep South, where once gauchos, Indians and military men fought their last battles or their last duels. 'Loneliness was perfect and perhaps hostile and Dahlmann could begin to suspect that he was not only going south but also towards the past.' Some abnormal details, like 'small displacements', begin to affect this almost perfect happiness: the train does not stop at the usual station and Dahlmann gets off in an unknown place, where he is told that it will be possible for him to get by car or carriage to his estancia. Dahlmann, says Borges, accepts this alteration 'as a small adventure'.[10] He reaches a *pulpería* where he observes several gauchos who remind him of the doctors and nurses that had taken care of him during his illness. Reality is blurred by parallelisms and coincidences, but nothing uncanny arises at first sight from this blurring. Dahlmann interprets these small changes, strange recognitions or misrecognitions, and displacements of light as something that is happening independently of his will to change or accept it. He surrenders to the unknown and expansive course of his destiny. Sitting at a table in the *pulpería,* waiting to be served his dinner, observed by gauchos who do not belong to present time (the story takes place in 1939 and these gauchos wear nineteenth-century dress), but who nevertheless do not seem out of place, Dahlmann dines on sardines, barbecued beef and strong red wine.

'All of a sudden Dahlmann felt something brush lightly against his face next to the heavy glass of turbid wine, upon one of the stripes in the tablecloth, lay a spit ball of breadcrumb. That was all: someone had thrown it there.' Clearly Dahlmann is being provoked, though nobody ought to know who he is, or at least that is what he thinks till he hears his name: 'Señor Dahlmann, don't pay any attention to those lads; they're half high'.[11] Dahlmann decides that, now that he has been recognized, he can no longer ignore the offence and avoid the conflict, because people would say that he had behaved as a coward in front of a bunch of drunken gauchos.

The certain knowledge that he should fight is at once clear, unavoidable and absurd. Somebody in the *pulpería*, a very old gaucho, throws a knife at his feet; Dahlmann grasps it and goes out into the night to fight a duel — so facing his South American destiny. 'It was as if the South had resolved that Dahlmann should accept the duel.'[12] When he bends down to take the knife, he feels that 'that an almost instinctive act bound him to fight' and that 'the weapon in his torpid hand was no defence at all but would merely serve to justify his murder'. Nevertheless, the story ends: 'Firmly clutching his knife, which he perhaps would not know how to wield, Dahlmann went out into the plain.'[13]

Like Martín Fierro in 'The End', Dahlmann is accepting his fate. But unlike Martín Fierro, who cannot help but act according to the only moral code he knows, Dahlmann has constructed this fate through making small choices among all the possibilities offered him by his dual origin: he was not born in the rural criollo world, he simply chose it following a whim that turned out to be fate. As in the story of the captive Englishwoman who decides to return to the Indian village and rejects the sympathy of Borges's grandmother, when Dahlmann goes south, he has begun to accept a part of his heritage, that of his grandfather Francisco Flores. In fact, when he thinks he is going south, to the estancia, to recover his health, he is really going south to recover an image of his past. This is the meaning, also, of the 'slight anachronisms': the gauchos dressed in nineteenth-century garb, the very primitive surroundings, the old man, a symbol — 'a cipher', writes Borges — who offers his knife to Dahlmann, guiding him towards his destiny: the acceptance of a tradition, but also the acceptance of death.

These details can clearly be seen as the hallmarks of fantastic literature: ambiguity of time and space, false recognitions or mis-recognitions, parallelisms and blurred references. But that is obvious. What I am trying to do here is to organize them into a 'theoretical' pattern which can reveal the meaning and the place of Argentine culture, and the ways in which one has access to its core and to its very menacing truth.

Like the captive English woman, Dahlmann is seized by the symbolic strength of primitivism, because what might be thought as primitive corresponds to a set of values and traditions (respect for fate, acceptance of destiny, physical courage) that are lacking in modern culture. In both stories, the criollo or Indian dimension takes revenge upon urban and literate spaces. In both, the main characters are reconquered through the fascination which barbarism exerts over them. Dahlmann, the librarian who seeks in the South something more than just the recovery of his health, accepts the incomprehensible criollo duel with a stranger for no reason, or at least for no reason he could name. The English captive chooses to return to the native settlement, swept away by, 'a secret impulse, an impulse more profound than reason'.[14]

Literature works with the material of this impulse which also guides Borges in his poetic invention of *las orillas*, the frontier between city and country, or between two worlds: Europe and Latin America, books and *caudillos* or *compadritos*, his English ancestors and his criollo blood. Something in the Argentine past is deeply linked to this rural culture, which Borges contrasts to the urban, literate and European tradition. Neither of these two lineages can be completely repressed or abolished; neither should be emphasized to the point of obliterating the other. Their coexistence results, however, not in any classical symmetry but in conflict.

The tension created by this double origin is at the heart of Argentine literature. It inhabits Dahlmann, who is capable of quoting stanzas of *Martín Fierro* by heart, as well as of appreciating a rare or remarkable edition of the *Arabian Nights*. Both books, we know, fascinated Borges. Both offer him a matrix for an infinity of stories, that can be read and reread in order to be rewritten in new texts. The *Arabian Nights*, needless to say, is also a translation, the form assumed by a classic Oriental text in a European language. In a way translation is also the problem of Latin American literature, at least from Borges's point of view: his country is a marginal space compared with the Western literary tradition, and the position of its writers is in itself problematic. The fact that they do not recognize a cultural fatherland in Spain leads them to connect their national literature with those of other European countries. But the fact that there is also a local cultural tradition does not simplify this connection. For years Borges worked on this problem in an allegorical and somewhat ironical way. Like Dahlmann, he knows his *Martín Fierro* by heart (and has re-written some of its episodes); like Dahlmann he values his criollo heritage; like Dahlmann he mixes this heritage into a European blend. He knows that the criollo past should not be looked for but found, should not be adopted but received — and this conviction gives him an opinion, too, about the integration of recent immigrants into Argentine culture.

'The South' is both tragic and ironic. It carries a double warning: cultural mixture may be our fate, but there is danger in it. One of the dangers is the bland romanticization of the criollo past that leads to a kind of rural literature, based on the picturesque, which Borges refutes and avoids in his fictional and critical practice. He writes: 'Blind to all fault, destiny can be ruthless at one's slightest distraction.'[15] The sentence may point to Dahlmann's distracted state of mind as he climbs the steps to his house, but it may also be read as an ironic anticipation of his fate. Distracted by the picturesqueness of the rural setting he has stumbled upon, Dahlmann cannot resist the allure of a criollo ending for his life, which can be looked upon not only as fate but also as a punishment for his Bovarism. Both meanings are equally possible in the multilayered irony of the story.

Borges's pattern for Argentine literature could be described as the European ordering of an American heritage rather than the predominance of local traits over European or imported culture. My reading of 'The South', has attempted to present, in its allegorical terms, this cultural mixture which never offers a happy ending but rather leads to conflict. The death of Dahlmann is significant not only because it is staged under the sky of the pampas and in a criollo duel (a peripeteia prefigured in *Martín Fierro*), but also because a librarian and the grandson of a European Protestant pastor is the man through whom destiny is thus fulfilled. Dahlmann, says Borges, cultivated a 'voluntary but never ostentatious *criollismo*' which was appropriate to a man of the city and reader of the *Arabian Nights* — a stranger, after all, to the archaic dimension (perhaps produced by his delirium) of the poor *pulpería* where he was to receive the summons to a duel. The fulfilment of this heterogeneity (a true oxymoron, as is the fair blue-eyed Indian woman) refers not only to the double origin of Dahlmann and of Borges, but of Argentine culture itself.

Mixture is at once indispensable and problematic. Borges is very far from the peaceful synthetic solutions which would turn Argentina into the idyllic space of a cultural melting-pot. On the contrary, all his literature is riven with feelings of nostalgia, because it takes place on the limit between two worlds, on a line which separates and joins them, but which, through its very existence, marks the insecurity of the relationship. In this sense, Borges's literature belongs to a frontier between Europe and America; it reveals distances and transformations, in the same way in which the inscription of writing separates the spaces of the page from the spaces of life.[16]

Notes

1. 'Dulcia Linquimus Arva', in J.L. Borges, *Selected Poems, 1923–67.* London 1972, pp. 49–51.

2. Leopoldo Lugones, *El payador*, Buenos Aires n.d.

3. J.L. Borges, *El hacedor*, Buenos Aires 1960, p. 38.

4. All these quotations are from 'The End', in J.L. Borges, *A Personal Anthology*, London 1972, pp. 137–8.

5. 'Biography of Tadeo Isidoro Cruz', in *A Personal Anthology*, p. 132.

6. 'Story of the Warrior and the Captive', in *Labyrinths*, London 1970, pp. 161–2.

7. Ibid., p. 159.

8. Ibid., p. 160.

9. 'The South' in *A Personal Anthology*, p. 13.

10. Both quotations, ibid., p. 15.

11. For both quotations, ibid., pp. 16–17.

12. Ibid., p. 17.

13. Ibid., pp. 17–18.

14. 'Story of the Warrior and the Captive', p. 162.

15. 'The South', p. 12.

16. The phrase is from Edward Said, *Beginnings*, New York 1986, p. 237.

FOUR

Tropes of
Fantastic Literature

Borges's fantastic fictions are considered one of his major claims to literary fame. Beginning in the sixties, in fact, his short stories have been read as the ultimate mise-en-scène of many of the problems that interest literary criticism. Both his fantastic stories and his fantastic essays (by which I mean texts such as 'The Analytical Language of John Wilkins' or 'Investigation of the Writings of Herbert Quain') deal with at least three sets of questions which are at once both aesthetic and philosophical: the sources of literary material; the strategies through which plot and formal procedures construct an imaginary world or an argument; the relationship between language and representation. In a sense, Borges has anticipated many of the topics that absorb contemporary literary theory: the referential illusion, intertextual production and the equivocal nature of meaning.

Borges's fantastic short stories can be read from different theoretical standpoints. Some approaches have their origins in, or are guided by, Borges's opinions on the art and craft of fiction. Others, which do not contradict these readings but at the same time do not place them at the centre of interpretation, try to understand the meanings of his fantastic fiction in terms of what, very generally, might be called contemporary history. This will be my task in the next three chapters.

Borges constructed his ars poetica on a double basis. On the one hand was the need to devise perfect plots, like those he admired in writers such as Kipling and Stevenson, who served as models for an aesthetic discipline designed to avoid the chaotic and disorganized nature of reality as imitated by realistic literature. On the other hand lay the appeal of the freedom fantastic literature enjoys with respect to naturalistic representation, realist poetics and psychological verisimilitude.

Borges always preferred the short story to the novel as a genre, because in his opinion unnecessary details always weigh down the plot of the modern novel, which is inevitably haunted by the ghost of representation and referentiality. The novel, Borges thought, could not free itself from traces, no matter how slight, of the real. The length required by the rules of the genre was one of the causes of its weakness; the length of the novel, if compared to the short story, offered a formal limitation to its perfection. Thus Borges frequently spoke out against realism and referential verisimilitude and frequently stated his irritation at Russian literature or French realism and naturalism. He complained that Russian novels presented characters who always engage in contradictory and often ridiculous behaviour, such as committing suicide because they feel happy, or killing someone out of love: characters grounded in the sort of complex psychologies that any reader can easily discover in Dostoevsky (and in one of Borges's Argentine contemporaries: Roberto Arlt). Novels, argued Borges, focused on characters instead of plot, and thus tended to a disorderly presentation of action which valued psychological insight over formal perfection. On the subject of *Ulysses*, the touchstone of contemporary fiction and a watershed for young writers in the thirties, Borges would state that he valued Joyce's magnificent *écriture* but that he had not been able to follow it from beginning to end. He had read parts of it, but never read it through completely. The statement should not be taken at face value, but it has to be considered as an aesthetic position with regard to *Ulysses*, and more generally with regard to modern and avant-garde literature. We should add, however, that Borges's translation of the last pages of Molly Bloom's monologue is, without doubt, the best translation of Joyce ever achieved in Spanish.

Borges had loved adventure stories since childhood. (Stevenson is, in this respect, the name that always comes to his lips, along with *The Arabian Nights*.) The pleasure to be derived from them depended on a well-wrought plot with no loose threads and little reference to deep psychological motives and impulses. Moreover, adventure novels do not face the problem of 'length', which for Borges always led to a weak plot, because they are generally organized into episodes that begin and end within the span of a chapter. Borges's consistent admiration for Stevenson and Kipling can be understood from this perspective, but not from this perspective alone. In his preface to *Doctor Brodie's Report*, a book published in 1970 when Borges was at the apex of fame and universal recognition, he still insists on this admiration and states that he has been inspired by Kipling's form:

> Kipling's last stories were no less tormented and mazelike than the stories of Kafka or Henry James, which they doubtless surpass; but in 1885, in Lahore, the young Kipling began a series of brief tales, written in a straightforward manner, that he was to collect in 1890. Several of them ... are laconic masterpieces. It occurred to me that what was conceived and carried out by a young man of genius might modestly be attempted by a man on the borders of old age who knows his craft. Out of that idea came the present volume, which I leave to the reader to judge.[1]

A well-constructed plot is a moral imperative in the sense that it promises no more than literature should (at least) offer to its reader: the pleasure of formal perfection with little interference from the lived world. In fantastic literature Borges can outline a perfect order solely by the force of narrativity and, apparently at least, independently of social reality: fantastic fiction offers hypothetical worlds based on the powers of an imagination unfettered by the constraints imposed by representative aesthetics. The fantastic is a mode dependent solely on the inner necessity of the text. Although it could be argued that realistic literature also presents hypothetical worlds that differ from the fantastic only in the degree of probability of their hypotheses, Borges always liked to argue his case against realistic representation as if what was at stake was not merely a literary tradition or a difference between genres of discourse but rather the very ethics of literature.

These opinions of Borges's are well known, and he has repeated them time and again ever since the essays he first published in the literary journal *Sur* and the weekly magazine *El Hogar* in the 1930s. Borges buttresses the independence of fiction with moral and aesthetic arguments. A perfect plot, the avoidance of unnecessary details that entail disorder and impose undesirable local features on the story (though Borges adds many forkings and deviations to his own fictions) and an aesthetic stylization of the voices of the text — these are the rules that writers should follow, not only in order to achieve aesthetic quality but also in order to be faithful to their duty, which is, precisely, to respect the means whereby they produce literature.

These principles may be viewed, beyond Borges's own presentation of them in connection with his ars poetica, as an aristocratic reaction to a disorderly world that in the 1930s seemed to be tottering on the edge of irrationality. Borges's defence of a rationalist fantastic literature (like his defence of a rationalist detective story modelled on Chesterton) is a creative response to the irrationality into which Western civilization seemed to have fallen: the irrationality of fascism, communism — and of mass democracy, which disgusted Borges as much as authoritarianism. Although Borges himself would not agree with such an interpretation of his fantastic *oeuvre*, it is nevertheless possible to understand it as a highly indirect, coded, and allegorical response to irrationalism (a philosophical point of view that Borges himself never endorsed) and to the state of contemporary culture, which Borges, in an essay on Valéry, described as follows:

> To propose lucidity to men in a lowly romantic era, in the melancholy era of Nazism and dialectical materialism, of the augurs of Freudianism and the merchants of *surréalisme*, such is the noble mission Valéry fulfilled (and continues to fulfil).[2]

Borges is here defining the task that he has set himself, in a world he considers to be out of sorts and inorganic. The order of his fantasy has nothing in common with the surrealist imagination, the Dadaist rejection of aesthetic hierarchy, or the Expressionist use of exasperation and fragmented distortion. On the contrary, he offers worlds that are nightmarish but obsessively complete and organized in a disturbing regularity.

His fictions might also be read as a response (no matter how he tried to preserve literature as a space free from direct political opinion) not only to processes taking place in Europe, where the rise of fascism and the consolidation of a communist regime in the Soviet Union gave concern to liberal intellectuals, but also to the inroads of mass democracy in Argentina. Not that in the 1930s mass democracy was exactly thriving there, after a military coup d'état had taken place in the early thirties and the Radical Party, which represented the middle classes and fractions of the popular sectors, had been banned. But what did worry Borges and his friends in the intellectual elite was the massification of culture and society in a country like Argentina that had gone so swiftly down the road of economic and social modernization, witnessing a process of urban growth that had in twenty years changed Buenos Aires almost completely, transforming it into a modern city like those of Western Europe.

Borges's response could be seen as the imposition of a principle of order in an world where immigration, multilinguism, the new order constructed by the Radical Party which had governed from 1916 to 1930, the social unrest which followed the crisis of 1929, seemed together to spell the end of criollo hegemony over culture and society. In short, the country and the city where Borges was living in the thirties and forties was dramatically different to that of his childhood. In the face of these changes he proposed the literary invention of a past, in his first three books of poetry, and the literary reordering of a reality which was liable to become unbearable (as indeed it did, for Borges at least, a few years later under the Peronist regime of 1945–55). Such a historical reading of Borges's fictions has not yet been attempted, but it could well shed new light on the role of Borges himself as an intellectual, and not just as a writer. We shall return to this point later.

But there are other ways of reading Borges's fantastic literature that seem unavoidable. Philosophical readings here take pride of place.[3] It is possible to see many of his stories as fictions that speculate with philosophical ideas in the same way as other fantastic fictions develop scientific or psychological ideas. In this sense, Borges's stories are the narrative mise-en-scène of a question which is not posed overtly but which is presented, in the fiction, through the development of a plot. This does not mean that each story offers the solution to a problem, at least not what is commonly or philosophically considered to be an answer or a solution. Far from it: Borges's stories do not offer a philosophical treatment of an idea, but rather what could be called a *philosophical narrative situation.*

Borges created a type of fiction in which ideas are not discussed through the characters, nor presented to the reader for consideration over and above the enjoyment of an unfolding narrative plot. On the contrary, ideas are the very stuff of the plot, and they shape it from the inside. Ideas in Borges are not only necessary to the development of the plot (as they are, for instance, in such different writers as Tolstoy or Joyce), they are presented as the plot itself. His fiction is based on the examination of an intellectual possibility presented as a narrative hypothesis. But Borges does not limit the power of the philosophical narrative situation to his stories. Many of his essays also present an idea (or two contradictory ideas) through a strategy that always plays with the border between facts and fiction, by means of false attributions, displacements, open and hidden quotations, parody, the hyperbolic development of a philosophical proposition, the mixture of invention and knowledge, and false erudition.

'The Analytical Language of John Wilkins' is a well-known short fictional essay in which Borges presents a classification of languages which he assigns to 'a certain Chinese encyclopedia':

> ... animals are divided into (a) those that belong to the Emperor, (b) embalmed ones, (c) those that are trained, (d) suckling pigs, (e) mermaids, (f) fabulous ones, (g) stray dogs, (h) those that are included in this classification, (i) those that tremble as if they were mad, (j) innumerable ones, (k) those drawn with a very fine camel's hair brush, (l) others, (m) those that have just broken a flower vase, (n) those that resemble flies from a distance.[4]

This strange, uncanny sequence — to which Foucault dedicated a magnificent commentary in his introduction to *The Order of Things* — combines, in the same way as a fictional fantastic plot, heterogeneous elements that do not follow the rules and order of what is considered reality or the reality of known languages. This heteroclite statement of an order that according to usual intellectual criteria is not really an order is a perfect example of what I have called a philosophical situation, and not a classical exposition of a problem or an attempt to solve that problem.

It is, in fact, a *presentation*, by means of the very Borgesian fictional device of a false attribution to an unknown or unlikely book, of the impossibility of offering linguistic form to what we call reality. No language mirrors reality, although many attempts have been made to explain why the use of language is posited on its capacity to transfer into words an arrangement of objects in space and time that is, in itself, remote from the very nature of discourse because the order of reality and the order of discourse respond to different logics. In its hyperbolic form, the fake Chinese encyclopaedia mimics other more rational efforts that philosophers and linguists have made to explore the mechanism through which we apprehend reality and the ways in which we divide up the experiential continuum of time and space. All these modes, says Borges under the cover of the Encyclopaedia, are conventions, because 'there is no classification of the universe that is not arbitrary and conjectural. The reason is very simple: we do not know what the universe is'.[5]

In order to show this in its textual form, he chooses to present the most heterogeneous classification, one that respects no logical principle of exclusion and inclusion, no logical formation of groups, species and genres and, above all, one that includes itself in the classification. This textual form is what I have called a philosophical situation.

The same could be said of what Borges calls the Aleph: a point that includes all the times and all the spaces of the universe, an abstract and at the same time concrete sphere where they are contained. It cannot be grasped through 'normal' perception because it encloses infinity, but it can be written. The Aleph suggests a philosophical dilemma: if it contains everything and every moment, then it should contain itself, but if it contains itself, then again, it must contain another Aleph that contains the previous two and so on, to infinity. Borges writes: 'I saw the Aleph from every point and angle and in the Aleph I saw the earth and in the earth the Aleph and in the Aleph, the earth'.[6]

> I owe to an old tin biscuit box my first notion of the problem of infinity. On one side of that abnormal object a Japanese scene was represented; I can't remember the children or the warriors that were depicted in it, but I do remember that on one corner of that image, the same tin biscuit box reappeared with the same scene on its side, and on it again the same scene and so on (at least potentially) endlessly.[7]

This is one of Borges's preferred visual arrangements of images: the *structure en abîme*, which is at the same time a narrative structure, a trope and a spatial model. The *structure en abîme* is another extraordinary example of what I have called a philosophical narrative situation: it poses a philosophical question (about infinity or infinite periodic repetitions) in terms of visual representation or in terms of a pattern for plots. It leads to what Bioy Casares, apropos of 'Tlön, Uqbar, Orbis Tertius', describes as a metaphysical fiction. The *structure en abîme* also engages with a topic of Western classical philosophy, the principle of identity, and it troubles us in a way that no other conceptual pattern does, because it asserts, to a degree, the superiority of images over reality:

> The inventions of philosophy are no less fantastic than those of art: Josiah Royce, in the first volume of his work *The World and the Individual* (1899), has formulated the following: 'Let us imagine that a portion of the soil of England has been levelled off perfectly and that on it a cartographer traces a map of England. The job is perfect; there is no detail of the soil of England,

no matter how minute, that is not registered on the map; everything has there its correspondence. This map, in such a case, should contain a map of the map, which should contain a map of the map of the map, and so on to infinity.'

Why does it disturb us that the map be included in the map and the thousand and one nights in the book of the *Thousand and One Nights*? Why does it disturb us that Don Quixote be a reader of the *Quixote* and Hamlet a spectator of *Hamlet*? I believe I have found the reason: these inversions suggest that if the characters of a fictional work can be readers or spectators, we, its readers or spectators, can be fictitious.[8]

The *structure en abîme*, by means of a baroque organization of space, establishes an order that is in itself a visual paradox; it compels us to imagine spatial infinity in a non-infinite space. According to the principle of endless inclusion, it modifies our belief in the truth of our perceptions and sets up a tension between what can be conceived logically and what can be concretely or materially or sensorily perceived. It corrects what Borges would describe as the imperfect nature of the world apprehended through the human senses. Like a well-drawn labyrinth, it is endless and, like a labyrinth, it sets up against the order of the world, which is impossible to discern, the conceptual order of a trope that corrects the imperfect notions that 'realistic' thought has fostered. The notion of endless circularity is present in labyrinths as well as in mirrors and in dreams that include other dreams or the dreamer. These mutually dependent structures that have no resolution, as logical dilemmas have no answer, exert a critical effect (they are methodological) on a metaphysical dimension. Thus the dreamer in 'The Circular Ruins' is wounded in his being by the circularity of dreams that, in a *structure en abîme*, include each other. Thus, too, in a Chinese story that Borges quoted many times, 'Zhuang Zi dreamt that he was a butterfly and he did not know when he awoke if he was a man who had dreamt of being a butterfly or a butterfly that was now dreaming of being a man'.[9]

We have already mentioned that Borges upholds perfection of plot as one of the principal rules of short fiction. He finds in the work of Kafka an example of this perfection, in its simplicity and in the nightmarish accumulation of minor and uncertain details and of repetitions. Borges analysed Kafka's novels in essays written in the late thirties. He argues that *The Trial* and *The Castle* obey the same logical mechanisms as Zeno's paradoxes, especially the paradox of Achilles and the Tortoise, which Borges loved, and evoked many times.

Achilles runs ten times faster than the tortoise and gives the animal a headstart of ten metres. Achilles runs those ten metres, the tortoise one; Achilles runs that metre, the tortoise runs a decimetre; Achilles runs a decimetre, the tortoise runs a centimetre; Achilles runs a centimetre, the tortoise, a millimetre; Fleet-footed Achilles, the millimetre, the tortoise, a tenth of a millimetre, and so on to infinity, without the tortoise ever being overtaken.[10]

In Kafka's novels the paradox is posed in terms of the impossibility of reaching the castle or of acquiring some knowledge which is vital to the protagonists. No matter what the characters in the novel try to achieve, there will always be another obstacle to overcome. Kafka organizes the fictional events in a sequence that can be infinitely divided and, for this reason, is spatially and temporally endless.

Borges admires paradoxes not for their incongruity with regard to experience but for their ironical demonstration of the force and limitations of logic. Paradoxes do not deal with inconsistencies or contradictions, but rather, through flawless formal consistency, they display how limited the mind is when it tries, on the one hand, to apprehend the nature of reality, and, on the other hand, to organize an ideal pattern which could conceivably correspond to that reality. Paradoxes have the virtue of displaying the limits against which literature (or philosophy) is constructed.

Paradox affects the principle of identity and, even more radically, the logical structure of our reasoning, demonstrating both that reasoning's possibilities (for anything can be logically demonstrated) and its strange mixture of strength and weakness in the face of reality (because what is demonstrated flies in the face of common sense). The fact is that paradox criticizes common sense and empiricism. The question, which perhaps cannot be answered, is whether paradox upholds the power of logic against the power of common sense, or, on the contrary, shows up the hollow nature of our reasoning, while pointing at the same time to the unavoidable conclusion that reality can be grasped neither through perception nor through the formal structure of logic. I think that both these answers are present at the same time in Borges's philosophical stories, whose power resides in the way he moves between two different requirements, the splendour of logical constructions and the despair aroused by a formal perfection that by definition cannot translate the unknown structure of the real world.

Paradoxes offer excellent material for the construction of fiction. Borges uses this logical trope along with others, which help him to demonstrate the infinite possibilities of various logical and formal combinations with no claim to a mimetic link with reality. On the contrary, formal and logical tropes are independent of the order of reality, which cannot be grasped in itself but only presupposed by and in thought. On several occasions Borges quoted from the thirteenth-century Spanish thinker Raimundo Lullio, inventor of a thinking machine (not a machine that was able to think, but a machine that could be used for thinking). Borges states:

> It [the machine] does not work, but that, to my mind, is a secondary matter. Nor do the machines that attempt to produce continuous movement, whose plans add mystery to the pages of the most effusive encyclopaedias; metaphysical or theological theories do not work either ... but their well-known and famous uselessness does not reduce their interest.[11]

However, Lullio's machine has, for Borges, what could be called an aesthetic productivity. And here we should remember that Borges, like the sages in Tlön,[12] judges metaphysical systems from the standpoint of their formal consistency and intellectual beauty. Lullio's machine is, symbolically, a sort of oxymoron or contradiction, because it was conceived to work out the solution of any problem through the methodical application of chance. Thus the conception of the machine is in itself an oxymoron, as it contradicts the idea of the 'machine' (which is opposed to haphazard results) and the idea of progressive stages towards the solving of a problem (although science today recognizes a more powerful impact of chance in the logic of research).

The machine consists of three revolving and concentric disks each with fifteen or twenty divisions. The divisions can be engraved with symbols, words, numbers or colours. Let us imagine, says Borges, that we want to know the true colour of tigers. We proceed to assign to each symbol or number on each disk a colour, and then turn the disks over in order to arrive at an arrangement produced by chance (or, if preferred, destiny). The signs on one disk will correspond to the signs on the others, establishing a kind of arbitrary syntax where we should be able to decipher that the true colour of tigers is, let us say, blue, yellow and gold, or yellowy blue, or goldish yellow or bluey gold, and so on. This extreme ambiguity is one more virtue of the machine, a virtue that could be multiplied if more than two machines were combined and put to work together. Borges concludes that for a long time, many believed that, if patiently manipulated, the disks could yield all the answers to every problem and 'the sure revelation of the arcane nature of the world'.[13]

What fascinates Borges is the oxymoronic nature of Lullio's invention, which I have already pointed out. He is also fascinated by the hyperbolic combination of haphazard responses which in their disparate union mirror the chaotic nature of reality, which can only be reordered by form, without the vain hope that this order can manage to represent or reproduce the real. The accidental responses we may obtain from the machine, though unmotivated and produced by chance, are nonetheless formally exact. The machine is precise, even if its precision has nothing in common with scientific method or with common sense and experience. It works according to the rules of fate, which are unknown to man, and its results should be read without violating the conventions accepted before the disks were set in motion (that is to say, without changing the conventional meaning of the letters or symbols painted on the disk's divisions).

One of the philosophers Borges often quoted in the thirties was Mauthner, and his account of Lullio's machine is distinctly reminiscent of Mauthner's definition of a rhyme dictionary as a machine for thinking where the rhymes of a word lead to other words, which come to be combined in a hypothetical poem only by phonetic necessity and semantic chance — chance belonging to an order required by form. And such a *necessary chance* is, in any event, an oxymoron.

Machines of this kind produce a formal proliferation which has to be respected and the rules of which (how to operate the machine and read its results) have to be followed. In the face of what seems a chaotic reality, literature should work with the same precision and severity as Lullio's machine: 'Every episode in a well-crafted story', wrote Borges, 'has an ulterior projection' — just as every movement of the disk modifies the elements present in the other three disks, and this modification should never be overlooked. No matter how strange the events told in a story, they should appear *as if* order were possible in the realm of the text.

In a remarkable parable, 'Inferno, I, 32', Borges has written:

Years later, Dante was dying in Ravenna, as unjustified and as lonely as any other man. In a dream, God declared to him the secret purpose of his life and work; Dante, in wonderment, knew at last who and what he was and blessed the bitterness of his life. Tradition relates that, upon waking, he felt that he had received and lost an infinite thing, something he would not be able to recuperate or even glimpse, for the machinery of the world is much too complex for the simplicity of men.[14]

The tropes of reason, the logical imagination, the rhetorical figures that point to the unavoidable contradiction between thought or discourse and reality, these were the ways in which Borges's fantastic fictions staged his despair in the face of Dante's illumination. But at the same time they are tools of reason, opposed to an irrationality to be felt not only in the texts of philosophers but also in the fabric of modern life itself.

Notes

1. J.L. Borges, *Doctor Brodie's Report*, London 1976, p. 11.

2. 'Valéry as Symbol', in *Labyrinths*, London 1970, p. 233.

3. An excellent study of Borges's philosophical sources can be found in Jaime Rest, *El laberinto del universo*, Buenos Aires 1976; on Borges's fantastic literature, see Ana María Barrenechea's seminal work, *La expresión de la irrealidad en la obra de Borges*, Buenos Aires 1967.

4. 'The Analytical Language of John Wilkins', in *Other Inquisitions*, Austin (Texas) 1964, p. 103.

5. Ibid., p. 104.

6. 'The Aleph', in Jorge Luis Borges, *The Aleph and Other Stories 1933-1969*, London 1973, p. 21.

7. 'Cuando la ficción vive de la ficción', in *Textos cautivos; Ensayos y reseñas en 'El Hogar' 1936-1939*, Barcelona 1986, p. 325.

8. 'Partial Magic in the *Quixote*', *Labyrinths*, pp. 230-31.

9. J.L. Borges and Adolfo Bioy Casares, *Cuentos breves y extraordinarios*, Buenos Aires 1986, p. 27.

10. 'Avatars of the Tortoise', *Labyrinths*, p. 237.

11. J.L. Borges, 'La máquina de pensar de Raimundo Lullio', in *Textos cautivos*, p. 177.

12. For a reading of 'Tlön, Uqbar, Orbis Tertius', see next chapter.

13. 'La máquina de pensar de Raimundo Lullio', p. 177.

14. *Labyrinths*, p. 273.

FIVE

Imaginary Constructions

We shall now attempt to read three stories, 'Tlön, Uqbar, Orbis Tertius', 'The Library of Babel' and 'The Lottery in Babylon', analysing their narrative organization through the tropes and rhetorical figures outlined in the previous chapter. We should be able to construct some meaning from the model of imaginary worlds these stories develop by describing the form and rules of their fictional order. We will bring apparently disparate lines of argument together into a hypothesis on the way in which Borges, by means of philosophical narrative situations, challenges the very nature of order. The questions that underlie these stories point to one of Borges's most complex problems: how can a chaotic world be converted into an order, although this order could result in a nightmarish organization? By organizing chaos, fictional order reveals a utopian (or rather a dystopian) world.[1]

Literary critics[2] have pointed out that the narrative and spatial design of 'Tlön, Uqbar, Orbis Tertius' is similar to a *structure en abîme*. According to an entry in the *Anglo-American Cyclopaedia*, Uqbar is a land vaguely located in Asia whose frontiers are marked by rivers and mountains of the same region (of Uqbar). This amounts to no definition at all, because the bounding landmarks are included in the space they should delimit, and refer to no other known country (an eloquent spatial presentation of a logical paradox). Tlön is an imaginary and mythical region in a land, Uqbar, that later on also proves to be an imaginary geographical and cultural construction. As the plot unfolds, Tlön becomes a planet invented by a sect by means of language alone. Finally,

Orbis Tertius is the world described in terms of the language spoken on an imaginary planet, Tlön, which has in turn been described previously as a mythical region of a dubious country, Uqbar. This closely knit sequence of non-existent lands and regions evokes the *en abîme* structure. It is easy to recognize the presence here of multiple images, as in a mirror reflecting a mirror.

At the beginning of the story Borges writes: 'I owe the discovery of Uqbar to the conjunction of a mirror and an encyclopedia'.[3] The mirror has been mentioned by his friend Bioy Casares, citing a heresiarch from Uqbar as having declared that mirrors and copulation were 'abominable because they increase the number of men'. The quotation begins the search for the *Anglo-American Cyclopaedia* (which, as Borges reports, is a reprint of the *Encyclopaedia Britannica*: an exact, or maybe not altogether exact, copy). Here Borges cleverly brings together two objects, the mirror and the encyclopaedia, both of which can construct *en abîme* images: the encyclopaedia is a conceptual mirror of a world whose classification may also include the notion of an encyclopaedia, and it may be thought of as a verbal and alphabetical Aleph.

The story presents, in a tangled fashion which is rather difficult to follow, the following narrative events (which I have reordered by year):

1935 One evening, Bioy Casares mentions to Borges a land called Uqbar about which he has been reading in a volume of the *Anglo-American Cyclopaedia*. An edition happens to be in the suburban house they have temporarily rented, but after consulting it they find that there is no entry for Uqbar. Bioy Casares insists that he has read about it in the *Cyclopaedia* and some days later he produces a volume which looks similar to the one they had consulted, except that it has four extra pages, which contain the article on Uqbar. The information given is vague, and Tlön is named as a mythical region of Uqbar.

1937 or 1938 Borges finds the eleventh volume of *A First Encyclopaedia of Tlön*, which has been sent to Herbert Ashe, a man whom he has met several times in a suburban hotel. This volume, whose first page is stamped with an oval bearing the inscription 'Orbis Tertius', has precious information about Tlön, much of which Borges presents as philosophical narrative situations in the story.

1941 A letter is discovered from Gunnar Erfkord to Herbert Ashe in which the enigma of Tlön is partially resolved. At the beginning of the seventeenth century a secret society conceived of the task of inventing a land. Each member of the sect had to elect a follower in this, in principle, endless or almost endless enterprise. After two hundred years of silent, or secret or interrupted operations, the society reappears in America. In 1824 one of its members recruits a millionaire who is enthusiastic about the project and proposes the more ambitious plan of inventing not just a land but a planet. At last, in 1914, the society is able to publish the final volume of the *First Encyclopaedia of Tlön*; it was now intended that this first edition would provide the basis for a revision, but one written this time in one of the languages of Tlön. This projected revision of an imaginary world is given the name of Orbis Tertius (the Third World: a phrase which had none of its current resonances when Borges wrote his story). The volume sent to Herbert Ashe and found by Borges in 1937 belongs to this new version of the encyclopaedia.

1942   Very strange objects, from Tlön, begin to appear in Argentina of all places: they are very heavy and Borges and one of his friends find one of them in a remote rural saloon in the pampas.

1944   A journalist in Nashville discovers the forty volumes of the *First Cyclopaedia of Tlön*. Borges writes a postscript which ventures the hypothesis that all countries and languages are bound to disappear and that the real world will become Tlön.

These are the 'facts' of the plot, what could be seen as the external history of the discovery of Uqbar. I have reordered and simplified Borges's much more complex sequence of events. Borges orders this material through two of his favourite devices: false attributions to a mixture of existing and invented texts, and the introduction of many of his real-life friends. Thus the borders between what really happened, what could have happened and what could never happen are interwoven by means of a method of verisimilitude which gives status to an invention with the name of a real existing person, and attributes to books whose nature is ambiguous (they could exist, they appear to be existing books) the origin of a fabulous situation or a necessary quotation. Needless to say this method of attribution and verisimilitude puts the status of reality in question; it also points to the permeable nature of fiction, which longs to grasp something that forever escapes it.

Let us turn now to the fictional information about Uqbar and Tlön. The story chooses to present a Tlönic conception of the universe, describing its language and the nature of its psychology — the only science deemed possible and worthwhile. Philosophers in Tlön have developed an extreme version of idealism, and the name of Berkeley appears as a fleeting reference before the multiplicity of hypotheses that make up the core and the originality of Tlönic thought are described:

> The fact that every philosophy is by definition a dialectical game, a *Philoso-phie des Als Ob*, has caused them to multiply. There is an abundance of incredible systems of pleasing design or sensational type. The metaphysicians of Tlön do not seek for the truth or even for verisimilitude, but rather for the astounding. They judge that metaphysics is a branch of fantastic literature. They know that a system is nothing more than the subordination of all aspects of the universe to any one such aspect.[4]

Narrative situations can be developed through the use of this 'as if' structure: to conceive the world *as if* it were a library, fate and destiny *as if* they were the form of order, as in 'The Library of Babel' and 'The Lottery in Babylon'. The 'as if' allows the deployment of a consistent invention (the kind of rational imagination, or logical form of the fantastic, we find in Borges). The sages of Tlön develop 'as if' philosophies, not only in order to interpret the world but also in order to modify the way it is perceived and the way it exists for the inhabitants of Tlön. They perceive and judge time, space, substance and identity according to prevailing tendencies in philosophy. But the 'as if' methodological principle of philosophical invention is a mode that permits the proliferation of different versions of 'reality' (so long as they do not contradict some very basic laws of Tlön, namely that the universe is 'a series of mental processes which do not develop in space but successively in time', that is to say that space, and substance, do not persist in time). These versions are briefly presented by Borges in what turns out to be a central part of the story. What Borges proves here is that fiction can be constructed with materials not usually thought of as fictional. He constructs his plot in accordance with the principles he attributes to the sages in Tlön, so that here too it is the attraction and beauty of systems, their capacity for awakening wonder (for performing as philosophical narrative situations), that is the basis of their value.

This philosophical narrative situation also opens up the problem of the conditions and limits of knowledge and understanding: what can be apprehended is never the Universe or its laws, but rather a discursive pattern constructed by human beings and their laws. God's labyrinth cannot be grasped by human understanding (if a God or gods exist: Borges is agnostic); only labyrinths built by humans can be understood by the human mind. The construction of the imaginary land of Tlön (which is largely the invention of a group of philosophical schools) is an exercise in the imposition of an order which, no matter how bizarre it may seem, can be contemplated by the human mind thanks to its power to accept paradox. In other words we must consider ideas that run counter to common sense: paradox is an inverted mirror.

The fantastic order of the planet Tlön is a utopia that criticizes the empirical and referential disorder that Borges tries to avoid through the perfect plotting of his fictions. The imaginary order amounts to a fictional response to the philosophical question, but a response couched in aesthetic strategies that adopt some of the forms of this philosophical argument.

Very briefly, the main traits of Tlönic culture can be summarized as follows (a) Time does not exist. While one Tlönic school of thought asserts that we live in an eternal present, indefinite and not partitioned into past and future, another upholds that all time has already passed and that what we live in is only remembrance. (b) Identity, according to this conception, is unimaginable, because no substance extends its being through time: the idea of the Subject, as conceived by modern philosophy since Descartes, is thus profoundly undermined. (c) No other general categories could possibly exist in a world where the continuity of time or of substance is denied.

The sages of Tlön favour an idealistic world-view and everything in Tlön's culture presupposes philosophical idealism. Borges very carefully describes Tlönic linguistic and philosophic theories which in many cases conform to his own. The sages have imagined that there is no spatial continuity, that space is by definition discontinuous, and that a place or object in space is never the same if considered from the point of view of time. This also affects the logical principle of identity, and the way we are used to perceiving the world and judging its objects (we tend to think that the pencil we are using is the same pencil we used yesterday, because we find it more comfortable to presuppose this identity).

In Tlön notions such as cause and effect have no sense at all. If the principle of identity is affected, if there is no spatial or temporal continuity, then no link can possibly be established between signs and events: a lighted cigarette, smoke and fire are distinct moments in a sequence that are not bound together syntactically or hierarchically. Since, in Tlön, there is no possibility of conceiving abstract notions of identity and causality, the sciences as we define them are not possible. Instead, hundreds of philosophies grounded in the *als ob* principle flourish, beautiful systems that do not claim any link with an external referent. That is to say, they have the basic structure of fantastic literature. The *als ob* principle is one of the possible strategies of utopian and dystopian fiction, where an 'as if' hypothesis launches the invention of a narrative. Thinking of time and space as discontinuous instead of continuous is the basic world-view of Tlön and it also permits the invention of an imaginary space according to rules that are grounded in an *als ob*.

Logically enough the two languages in Tlön have no nouns. One is based on compound adjectives, the other on compound verbs. Nouns are in principle impossible, because there is no continuous substance that can provide the empirical/logical basis for a noun. What we consider nouns come about in Tlön from the accumulation of adjectives indicating ephemeral states. Of course, this type of adjective can be used only once, because by definition no state can repeat itself in time.

The same happens with certain verbs, like 'to find' and 'to lose'. Both actions are inconceivable in Tlön because, if there is no identity between objects and no continuity in space and time, no object can be lost, much less found again. When something that we would consider 'to be lost' happens to an object, a kind of secondary object (vaguely different to the lost one) begins to proliferate. These simulacra are called *hrönir* and they can be usefully employed to invent and modify the past, an activity that occupies and fascinates archaeology in Tlön. The existence of the *hrönir*, which every man in Tlön is used to, is a practical demonstration of the absence of any basis for the principle of identity that sustains our own culture. In an idealist planet like Tlön, a planet constructed by language, to lose means to forget and to find means to remember: both actions serve to produce *hrönir*.

In Tlön, to be exactly the same does not mean to be the same, because the principle of identity does not exist. Tlönic philosophies thus have no way of constructing the category of the Subject, which is central to Western philosophy in modern times. Moving on from this non-existence of the Subject, some literary critics in Tlön deal with the construction of the author, which is always hypothetical because they attribute different texts to the same author: 'They select two dissimilar works — the *Tao Te Ching* and the *1001 Nights*, say — attribute them to the same writer and then determine most scrupulously the psychology of this interesting *homme de lettres* . . .'[5] A strategy not unknown to Borges himself when he writes his 'fantastic' critical stories and essays.

Indeed, the dissolution of the category of the author and the attribution of very different texts to an invented *persona* is one of Borges's preferred versions of authorship in literature. Many of his short stories work with the idea that authorship is irrelevant, as we have seen in 'Pierre Menard, Author of the *Quixote*'. Menard's work is superior to that of Cervantes precisely because, since he is not a man of the sixteenth century, Menard is more original and startling than Cervantes, even though both texts (the Cervantes *Quixote*, the Menard *Quixote*) may *look* exactly the same. Menard's superiority is grounded in a discussion of the principle of identity.

Borges undertakes a similar Tlönic activity when he invents authors and writes short literary essays on them — essays which are in fact fantastic fictions. Such is the case of Herbert Quain, an imaginary writer whose imaginary books Borges describes in detail. Quain's fictions, by the way, are very similar in conception to the fictions of Tlön: they include all the possibilities of a plot, and all are explored in an infinity of bifurcations. For Quain, as for the sages of Tlön, 'a book that does not enclose its opposite should be considered incomplete': his ideal for the novel is to deploy every possibility contained in an argument; taken to its logical extreme, this ideal makes literature impossible, or at least highly problematical.

These fragments of Tlönic knowledge and learning are the philosophical core of Borges's story. But there is more to the philosophical situation presented in 'Tlön, Uqbar, Orbis Tertius'. As we have seen, the planet is a fantastic world invented by a secret sect that acts as a collective writer. The existence of Tlön is based on an *als ob* presupposition, which is itself based on the power of language to produce a reality, or at least what from an idealist point of view might be called a reality. Formed by language, Tlön has its origins in one of Borges's favourite forms of textuality: the encyclopaedia, in this case a pirate copy of Borges's beloved *Encyclopaedia Britannica*. It also emerges from the activity of a sect, an organizational form that also fascinated him. The *First Encyclopaedia of Tlön* is a textual utopia, the perfect realm of philosophical fiction. But, at the end of the story, Tlön begins to infect the imperfect reality in which we live: objects from Tlön cross the very thin line between a world of words, treated as such, because they are in an encyclopaedia, and a world of words treated as 'real' (in ironic inverted commas), because in this world readers can find mention of Borges, Bioy Casares and half a dozen other Argentine writers. The *als ob* where Tlön originates reveals the strength of the idealistic tenets of Tlönic wisdom, and objects from the *als ob* world begin to invade reality through a process of silent contamination.

Imaginary languages are at the centre of the philosophical narrative situation of this short story. In the original Spanish, while describing one of the two languages of Tlön, Borges mentions the imaginary language invented by his friend the painter Xul Solar, which was based on a kind of Esperanto syntax with a criollo and *porteño* vocabulary.[6] This language was clearly based on parody. These references, however ironic, allow us to chart Borges's interest in artificial and imaginary languages and systems of representation. In his view these are more fascinating than real languages because they have no muddled links with a reality which is by definition chaotic. John Wilkins, the invented character in one of Borges's fictional essays, which we have already cited, has for example divided up the universe into forty categories, designated by monosyllabic names each composed of two characters or sounds only. These categories, in turn, are subdivided into genres designated by an extra consonant sound; genres divided into species are indicated by a vocal sound. Volapuk is another artificial language evoked by Borges: invented by a German priest, its verbs can adopt any one of five hundred thousand forms, which include potential, imperative and subjunctive forms of the type 'peglidalod', meaning 'you should be greeted'. Volapuk was eventually replaced by Esperanto, based on Latin roots. Imaginary languages, though impossible to use, can be logically accurate because they have been consciously structured. And this gives them supremacy over what we know as natural languages, which are, by definition, a product of sociohistorical processes.

History, for Borges as for Joyce, can turn into a nightmare. The only antidote against its chaos, which mirrors the chaos of reality, is the activity of invention. Languages of the type found in Tlön do not mirror the world itself but rather an *idea of the world*. They work on a philosophical and not on a social or empirical basis. The languages of Tlön have a transparent relationship to the ideal concept of reality: they can never suffer from the disorder of experience. On the contrary, they shape experience.

But imaginary languages have other symbolic advantages. They not only prevent the chaos of experience from being transferred to thought and language. They also resist the social chaos that lies at the heart of any modern society. Real languages bear the marks of demographic mixture, especially in societies like those in Latin American countries such as Argentina, where the Spanish criollo population of colonial origin was replaced (by more than 50 per cent) by immigrants from South and Central Europe. These demographic changes, which Argentine intellectuals in the first third of this century considered dangerous from ideological, cultural, linguistic and political viewpoints, can be symbolically overridden by the abstract discipline of a philosophical and narrative situation.

This is, of course, an ideological account of Borges's fantastic story, and one with which he would have strongly disagreed. All the same it can be justified in social and historical terms; more important, it tallies with Borges's own preoccupations about national culture in the twenties, with his rereading of the national past and his rewriting of gauchesque literature. Borges, as we have seen, invented an image of Buenos Aires as a city untouched by migration and demographic complexity. The real Buenos Aires where he was living seemed chaotic and its heterogeneity menacing and unaesthetic. Although his main response to this experience was his creation of a Buenos Aires myth based on *las orillas*, it is by no means absurd to read such fantastic stories as 'Tlön, Uqbar, Orbis Tertius' as another strategy for establishing order for a society whose old orders were vanishing.

Borges often pointed out that Kafka's short stories (which he himself expertly translated), had plots of 'terrible simplicity', and he attributed their aesthetic impact to this quality. It is not a merely formal quality, and defines the story we shall consider next: 'The Library of Babel'. Borges called this story a 'Kafkaesque fiction'. Its main image, the Library, was inspired by his experience as a librarian in Buenos Aires, which the story describes, in Borges's words, through the lens of an 'oneiric magnification'.[7]

Even if we overlook these biographical minutiae and Borges's permanent fascination with the order and physical or ideal arrangement of books, the Library remains one of the central motifs in his fictions and poetry. The story begins with this motif, used as a metaphor:

The universe (which others call the Library) is composed of an indefinite and perhaps infinite number of hexagonal galleries, with vast air shafts between, surrounded by very low railings. From any of the hexagons one can see, interminably, the upper and lower floors. The distributions of the galleries is invariable. Twenty shelves, five long shelves per side, cover all the sides except two.[8]

This is the first, simple description of the hypothetical world developed as a narrative and as a spatial organization in the story. The Library is at once an ordered space and a labyrinth of a kind that Borges admires. It is geometrical, regular, with no tricks save in its very structure, based on a repetition of identical elements (the hexagon is a regular spatial figure with a harmonic symmetrical quality). As Borges himself declared in an interview,[9] his first spatial idea for the Library of Babel was to describe it as an infinite combination of circles, but he was annoyed with the idea that the circles, when put in a total structure, would have vacant spaces in between. He chose the hexagon for its perfect simplicity and its perceptive affinity to the circle.

The Library in Babel is endless and interminable, because a new hexagon can always be added to the open structure. But, as all the hexagons look the same, as they have the same number of shelves, the same type of entrance or exit, and as the books contained in the shelves have exactly the same number on each shelf of each wall of each hexagon, the infinity of the Library cannot be empirically experienced, even if a traveller were granted infinite time. It can only be conceived, and thus challenged, intellectually. There is no way to confirm it through practical knowledge: the infinity of the Library is a theoretical hypothesis or a matter of belief. Thus the philosophical question of the story is generated by the narrative mise-en-scène. In this connection Borges quotes Pascal without mentioning his name: 'The Library [Pascal: the universe] is a sphere whose exact centre is any one of its hexagons [Pascal: is everywhere] and whose circumference is inaccessible.'[10]

Structurally, the Library is also a panoptic, whose spatial distribution of masses and corridors allows one to see every place in it from any of its hexagons. The panoptic design of the Library brings to mind that of a prison where the guards should be able to see any cell from every possible perspective. Foucault has studied this layout as a spatialization of authoritarianism, as an image of a society where total control is possible and no private place (no private thought) is admitted. The universe described as the Library lacks any notion or possibility of privacy: all the activities are, by definition, public. 'To the left and right of the hallway there are two very small closets. In the first, one may sleep standing up; in the other, satisfy one's fecal necessities'.[11] And, by definition, all the activities must conform to the only possible practice in a Library: the search for a written meaning.

All the books in the Library look exactly the same: each of them has four hundred pages, each page forty lines, each line eighty characters. The inscriptions on the covers of the books do not indicate their content. We know that the number of possible characters is twenty-five and that they mostly combine, according to Borges, in a chaotic form. In some regions of the Library, the librarians think that it is absurd to try to find a meaning in these books, and that this activity is based merely on old superstitions. There are also philosophers in the Library who cultivate agnosticism and think that the books do not have any concealed or apparent meaning. Everybody knows that each book has no duplicate, that it is in itself an original. But it is also known that there are in existence an indefinite number of books that contain slight variations.

The hypothesis the story presents through its narrator is that the Library contains precisely everything. Borges offers one of his typical enumerations, combining heterogeneous elements into a *structure en abîme*:

> The minutely detailed history of the future, the archangels' autobiographies, the faithful catalogue of the Library, thousands and thousands of false catalogues, the demonstration of the fallacy of those catalogues, the demonstration of the fallacy of the true catalogue, the Gnostic gospel of Basilides, the commentary on that gospel, the commentary on the commentary on that gospel, the true story of your death, the translation of every book in all languages, the interpolations of every book in all books.[12]

As a consequence of the nature and contents of the books in the Library, Borges states that the solution of the 'basic mysteries of humanity' should be found there, but that four centuries have elapsed since men began looking for this solution without ever finding it. Today, adds Borges, 'nobody hopes to find anything'. The search, which is conducted in an infinite space full of infinite combinations, cannot be directed by method but must be directed by chance. Borges organizes his narrative according to the conflictual structure of the oxymoron: the method the Library requires is by definition the antithesis of method. The logic of the Library is planned in such a way that it cannot be grasped, and, since the Library is the universe, the logic of the universe is inaccessible. Everything is in the Library but nothing can be found.

Besides, the Library is a predestined universe for the very reason that everything, past, present and future (Borges writes with some pathos: 'the story of your death') is written somewhere, in a book that has little chance of revealing its contents. This unhappy prospect does not diminish, but rather emphasizes, predestination. Apart from agnostic philosophers and those who have fallen into despair, human beings know that their destiny is written, and that their lives have been organized, by the quest for a meaning that cannot be grasped. Life itself is tautological, because everything that can be performed, thought or said has in the past been written in one of the books of the Library. The fact that this book has not yet been found (or will never be found), does not blot out the certainty that if men's lives are written somewhere, then they cannot be changed. The same process of finding the key to all the 'mysteries of humanity', the way to reach that particular book, is also written; and the place of that book is marked in a catalogue. But the librarians know that this catalogue has not (and by definition could not) be found: nothing can be found in a universe that is boundless and periodic. As Borges states at the end of the story: 'If an eternal traveller were to cross it in any direction, after centuries he would see that the same volumes were repeated in the same disorder (which, thus repeated, would be an order: the Order).'[13] If this is true, the quest of humanity in the Library-universe is pointless. But nobody can establish the truth or falseness of an organization whose rules are secret until the moment somebody finds them in a book, and that moment is either impossible (because the books are randomly written and convey no message) or improbable (because the search takes place within the inexhaustible space of a labyrinthine and symmetrical architecture).

In this philosophical and narrative situation, life is either predetermined by laws which cannot be identified but which have forever defined an order that leaves no space for the introduction of change, or else society is randomly organized to the point where mere chance, the eccentricity of fortune (somebody, without reason, happens on the key-book), is as strong as a predetermined organization of the world. In either case, human beings are unable to change their place and destiny. In either case, the rules that govern the world are secret and concealed from its subjects. Both cases lead logically to a dilemma.

In 'The Lottery in Babylon',[14] the logical and rhetorical tropes (primarily paradox and oxymoron) which reveal the limits of reason in recognizing the shape of an order also structure the narrative situation. The story is told by an anonymous voice — perhaps that of an exile from Babylon, somebody who belongs to the city but who is telling the story elsewhere, somebody whose current situation is not explained in the text. The storyteller expresses a sharp nostalgia for the world he has abandoned, or has been expelled from: — 'Now, far from Babylon and its beloved customs' — and reveals that he is about to embark on a voyage whose destination is not, we conjecture, his native land: 'I don't have much time left; they tell us that the ship is about to weigh anchor'. This anonymous voice longs for what could be considered an atrocious and inhuman rule, one introduced by the lottery into all the domains of the lived world and experience, for, as he puts it, the lottery is 'an intensification of chance, a periodical infusion of chaos in the cosmos'.[15]

As in almost any part of the world, the lottery had begun in Babylon as the game we all know about. At the beginning of the century in Buenos Aires, the tickets were sold in barbers' shops and no major excitement was caused by the drawing of lots and its results. 'Their moral virtue', writes Borges, 'was nil. They were not directed at all of man's faculties, but only at hope'. The lottery adjudicated only prizes, and money was the only stake. But at some time in the past, somebody put in some unfavourable lots: playing in the game now meant not just the possibility of winning money but also of losing it, through monetary fines. Soon very few people agreed to pay them, and the Company that managed the lottery decided to replace the fines with imprisonment. Every loser chose this second form of penalty. As time went by, and the success of this form of negative betting grew, the Company (which is always named in this way, with a capital letter and with no other details) began to include other types of unfavourable lots: physical punishments of the utmost cruelty, such as losing a limb or a tongue or an eye, were added to the possibility of imprisonment. Soon the new type of lots began to govern every activity in Babylon and, more radically, it became impossible to distinguish between what had resulted from drawing a lot and what from other factors. For instance, a slave that had stolen a lottery ticket had to be punished for this act by having his tongue burned, but the ticket he had in his possession also won him the same punishment. It was impossible to decide if the slave's tongue was burnt for the first reason (robbery) or for the second (his fortune in the lottery game).

This equivocal nature of events seized the imagination of the Babylonians, and popular revolts won everybody the right to participate in the lottery without paying for the tickets, which henceforward were to be distributed equally. The Company was established as the supreme government and authority of the city. This democratization of the right to gamble can clearly be seen as an ironic commentary on the extension of civil rights in modern societies. The social upheaval that brought about universal and free rights to the lottery tickets, a sort of ironic French Revolution, guaranteed that any free man in Babylon had the right to participate in what was now considered the sacred ceremony of drawing the tickets, which took place every sixty nights and determined the fate of the participants until the next draw. Once so organized, life also became sacred, because fate openly ruled the city. Nevertheless, nobody could possibly decide which events in his own life originated in the draw and which were a result of his own action or will. The draws were complicated; they used a system of multiple possibilities, and mistakes were often made by the sages that drew the lots. But the Company defended its operation as the introduction of chance into the world order, asserting that 'to accept errors is not to contradict chance: it is to corroborate it'.

This brief plot summary leaves us with the question of what kind of fictional society is being described. It is a utopian order (if we accept that the narrator's longing for Babylon is sincere), but one that could be understood as producing dystopian conditions. As the anonymous voice recalls, the lottery had the effect of establishing a society that was at the same time authoritarian and equitable, because the social fate of each individual was determined by chance, not by birth or merit:

> Like all men in Babylon, I have been proconsul; like all, a slave. I have also known omnipotence, opprobrium, imprisonment. Look: the index finger on my right hand is missing. Look: through the rip in my cape you can see a vermilion tattoo on my stomach. It is the second symbol, Beth. This letter, on nights when the moon is full, gives me power over men whose mark is Gimmel, but it subordinates me to the men of Aleph ... During a lunar year I have been declared invisible. I shouted and they did not answer me; I stole bread and they did not behead me. I have known what the Greeks do not know, incertitude.[16]

This dystopian order is underpinned by a number of tropes and stylistic devices. In the first place there is the oxymoron, the trope that blends contradictory elements, and by means of which meaning is challenged or modified by its combination with another meaning. In the case of Babylon, the oxymoron (which gives a structure to the narrative) establishes the fact that society is founded on chance: order is governed by the principle of disorder.

This oxymoron is sustained by a paradox: in its final state, the lottery requires an infinite number of drawings in order to decide events that should occur in a limited period of time. The time for the drawings should be infinitely divisible, as (in the famous paradox of Zeno) the time needed by the tortoise to win its race against Achilles. The most terrible, just like irrelevant actions, demand the proliferation of drawings. If a man is to be killed, this has to be established by a drawing. Another man is his murderer, and this too must be decided by the lottery. The circumstances of the murder also have to be settled by the draw, as do the conditions that determine this act, and so on endlessly. This forking is potentially interminable, and requires a temporal lapse that can be divided infinitely.

These tropes (the oxymoron of an order established by chance, and the paradox of the infinite division of time in a determined lapse of time) organize the text and construct a hypothetical world, based on a philosophical dilemma: *chance has been abolished by chance*. Where everything is attributed to chance, chance becomes the natural and social order; chance is indeed no longer chance, but necessity. This implies that all attempts to interrupt the play of chance must also be attributed to chance. This rule has no limit and repeats itself *en abîme*. Babylon has produced an oxymoron as the pattern of social order: universal organized chance, abolishing all possibility of free will or self-determination.

It is not difficult to read this story allegorically, not only as a presentation of destiny, but as a presentation of totalitarianism in the order of everyday life. The name of Kafka is disguised in the text: Borges remarks in an aside that Babylonians who had complaints against the Company used to leave letters in a sacred latrine called Qaphqa (the phonetic transcription of Kafka's name in the form of an Arabic word).

As in Kafkaesque nightmares, the order of the world cannot be grasped by its subjects, and one questions not only the legitimacy of that order but also its very existence. This is precisely what some conjecture in Babylon: that the Company has never existed and will never exist. Or that, although the Company is all-powerful, it decides only on minor issues and leaves the rest to a different and unknown chance which is not the chance of the lottery. For example, writes Borges, the Company has influence only over 'a bird's call, in the shadings of rust and of dust, in the half dreams of dawn'. Or it organizes an impersonal drawing for secret reasons: 'One decrees that a sapphire of Taprobana be thrown into the waters of the Euphrates; another, that a bird be released from the roof of a tower; another, that each century there be withdrawn (or added) a grain of sand from the innumerable ones on the beach'.[17] These last heretical hypotheses are more terrible than the empire of fortune, because the consequences of such apparently minor acts cannot be foreseen or calculated.

However, nobody can judge the truth of these suppositions and rumours. The Company gives only vague explanations about its rules. The heretical thinkers have ideas that cannot be proved. The institution of social order is unknowable and it lies beyond the limits of experience. And, in what is a more terrible conclusion, it can be seen that societies obey no rules other than that of arbitrary fortune.

In his prologue, written in 1941, to the first edition of the book where these stories were published, Borges writes that '"The Lottery in Babylon", although fantastic, is not altogether innocent of conveying a symbol'.[18] In one of his typical asides, he points us in the direction of reading the story in terms of political fiction. Fascism was at its zenith, and European democracy and its party system had not been able to offer a political alternative to the rise of authoritarianism in the thirties. Both facts posed an open question, although the world war appeared as a violent resolution to the problem of fascist expansionism. Namely, what is a society? What is the form through which order can be established without entirely eliminating freedom? Is there any way of combining the self-determination of individuals with a reasonable regulation of society?

I must agree that these do not sound like very Borgesian questions. Nevertheless, no matter how obliquely, 'The Lottery in Babylon' deals with them, and not only because they were on the agenda of the thirties. I would reject any suggestion that Borges was working with a public agenda, although he was preoccupied by authoritarianism. The question of social order can, after all, be considered from a philosophical as well as a political point of view. In the great tradition of Western thought this question has in fact occupied both philosophers and writers. It is at the basis of novels like *Robinson Crusoe* and *Gulliver's Travels* — both much loved and much quoted by Borges. Since society is not a natural fact, it presents problems that affect the central nucleus of philosophical thought. Such topics include the definition of the subject, the necessary limits placed on the relationship between individuals that choose to live in a social order, the conflict between freedom and obligation, the moral dimension of politics and the moral basis of social institutions.

'The Lottery in Babylon' (and also, although it is more openly meta-physical, 'The Library of Babel') can be read not only as philosophical but also as political-philosophical fictions. As we have seen in the case of 'Tlön, Uqbar, Orbis Tertius', this does not mean that they discuss a philosophical problem in a systematic manner, but rather that they present it in a narrative situation. Political philosophy is not to be learnt from Borges. But he does invent plots where a philosophical question is confronted by means of fictional devices and processes. There is no answer to the question. What we find, instead, is the literary develop-ment of the problem in the form of a plot built around fictional hypo-theses that describe a utopian — or, in effect, a dystopian — order.

Notes

1. On the topic of order and chaos in Borges, see Ana María Barrenechea, *La expresión de la irrealidad en la obra de Jorge Luis Borges*, Buenos Aires 1967; Jaime Rest, *El laberinto del universo*, Buenos Aires 1976; and Sylvia Molloy, *Las letras de Borges*, Buenos Aires 1979.

2. In particular, Arturo Echavarría Ferrari, 'Tlön, Uqbar, Orbis Tertius', *Revista Iberoamericana*, 100–101, 1977.

3. 'Tlön, Uqbar, Orbis Tertius', *Labyrinths*, Harmondsworth 1970, pp. 27–43.

4. Ibid., p. 34.

5. Ibid., p. 37.

6. Describing one of the languages of Tlön, Borges writes (ibid., pp. 32-3): 'There are no nouns in Tlön's conjectural *Ursprache*, from which the "present" languages and the dialects are derived: there are impersonal verbs, modified by monosyllabic suffixes (or prefixes) with an adverbial value. For example there is no word corresponding to the word "moon", but there is a verb which in English would be "to moon" or "to moonate". The "The moon rose above the river" is *hlör u fang axaxaxas mlö*, or literally: "upward behind the onstreaming it mooned".' At this point, the original Spanish version adds: 'Xul Solar translates briefly: *upa tras perfluyue lunó*. Upwards, behind the onstreaming it mooned.' J.L. Borges, *Obras completas*, Buenos Aires 1974, p. 435.

7. Borges worked in city libraries during the forties and fifties and became the director of the National Library after the fall of Perón in 1955.

8. 'The Library of Babel', *Labyrinths*, p. 78.

9. Christina Grau, *Borges y la arquitectura*, Madrid 1989, p. 74.

10. 'Babel', p. 79.

11. Ibid., p. 78.

12. Ibid., pp. 81–2.
13. Ibid., pp. 83–4.
14. 'The Lottery in Babylon', *Labyrinths*, pp. 55–61.
15. All quotations, ibid., pp. 55–7.
16. Ibid., p. 55.
17. Both quotations, ibid., p. 60.
18. Prologue to *El jardín de los senderos que se bifurcan*, Buenos Aires 1941, reprinted in *Obras completas*, Buenos Aires 1974, p. 429.

SIX

The Question of Order

Fiction has the power to construct an order or a meaning in the face of a disorderly world, not only by interpreting reality by deciphering its hidden clues, after the fashion of Romantic ideology, but also by challenging its causal, spatial and temporal logic with a different type of pattern. In this sense, fantastic fiction, far from being a somewhat secondary discourse, stands as an independent response to reality. Fantastic fiction disturbs reality not through re-presentation but through contradiction or divergence. It stresses the tension present in the act of writing, as writing drifts away from realistic discourse, which is, of course, only one possible way of relating art to social life. Although reality and fiction obey different logics, at some point they intersect — as, for instance, when the reader of a text finds that a conflict arises between these two logics, that something in the logic of reality contradicts the logic of a text, or that the logic of a text appears to be more persuasive or consistent than that of reality.

When history seems to offer no sanctuary for values (when history is assailed by wars and inhuman or immoral public actions), literature can provide a model, often as horrendous as that of history, but one which by virtue of its fictional nature is bound to keep an ironic, parodic, aesthetic or philosophical distance from what is at risk in immediate experience or direct reflection.

Borges always withdrew from an open discussion of contemporary politics in his literature, yet the question of the ways in which order imposes itself on human communities can be found woven into the

80

fabric of his plots. Indeed, he is examining the ideological and cultural conditions of society even as he outlines imaginary worlds which legitimately belong to the purest tradition of fantastic literature. 'Tlön, Uqbar, Orbis Tertius', 'The Lottery in Babylon' and 'The Library of Babel', which we considered in the last chapter, offer alternative images of society. In fact they are nightmares that show institutional organization to be based on blind power, arbitrary rulings or myths. The question of the acceptance of order is often examined, as are the conditions which produce disorder when that order is for some reason weak or absent.

Borges has written a great deal on violence and individual revenge. His urban *orillero* stories and his reworking of the gauchesque tradition show individual violence to be necessary where a code of honour holds sway and where formal law has not established its domain. The idea of violence is deeply embedded in his version of criollo culture: it is lived as a South American destiny, which for decades has endangered society but which has also given it a consistent meaning. The public confrontation of two men in a duel, in a rite which both parties accept as law, refers us to values that could be judged barbaric but that, at the same time, uphold a degree of community where no state and no formal codes have successfully organized social relations. The duel defined not only what a society was, but also what it was not, demonstrating that no formal procedures were in place to offer an alternative to a confrontation between armed men who trusted in the code of honour to resolve their disputes or to uphold justice.

In the first half of the nineteenth century, Argentine society was suffering the effects of the Wars of Independence, which in overthrowing the old colonial order had unleashed rival forces that fought each other for decades before agreeing to a constitutional pact in 1853. Until then, especially in the countryside, individual or group violence coped with the tasks that a very weak state (or rather, a non-existent national state) could not carry out. Conflicts in regional governments were an obstacle to the imposition of formal procedures capable of transforming individual feuds into regulated conflicts. In this criollo world, the myth of personal courage was bound to take the place of other, more 'civilized', forms of public behaviour and their corresponding values.

Borges saw that this problem was a central issue of criollo culture. By exploring the myths of this culture, he indirectly pointed out that these myths came from, and were nourished by, a historical situation where society was weak, state institutions were absent, and consequently

conflicts were resolved through violence. In 'Poema conjetural' ('Conjectural Poem'), Borges imagines the last thoughts of Francisco Laprida,
the man who had signed the act of Argentine independence from Spain
in 1816. These thoughts reveal the contradiction between abstract
notions of justice and the concrete forms of criollo violence. In 1829,
during an extraordinarily acute period of civil war, Laprida is killed by
the *montoneros*, a gaucho warrior band whose members excelled in the
art of knife- and spear-fighting:

> And Francisco Narcisco de Laprida, I
> who studied canon law and civil,
> whose voice declared the independence
> of these harsh provinces, am overthrown,
> covered with blood and sweat,
> without fear or hope, lost,
> fleeing south through the farthest outskirts ....
>
> I longed to be something else, a man of
> sentiments, books, judgement,
> and now will lie in a swamp under the open sky.
> And yet, a secret joy inexplicably
> exalts me. I've met my destiny,
> my final South American destiny.[1]

Borges often pointed out that the criollo branch of his family had its
roots in this nineteenth-century Argentina, and that his great grand-
parents had possessed a knowledge related to a primitive world of
cattlemen and cavalry commanders that was ruled by custom and the
unwritten laws of violence: a sort of heroic, primitive, rural dystopia.
This was a society where the use of power and physical force had not
come under the sway of institutional regulation, much less of state
monopoly. Here, myths of courage and masculine endurance flourished
as the cultural response to a social environment. Such a society could
exist only if some form of virtue was seen in personal ties of dependence,
concrete services or obligations secured by traditional vows, and loyalty
to the *patrón* or to other leaders. Without this kind of bondage, rural
society (where state officials, if there were any, had less power than
private landowners) would have tended to dissolve into anarchy. This is
very probably one of the reasons for the long tradition of political insult
directed against modernizers in nineteenth-century Argentina. The
modernizing fraction were labelled as anarchist, heretical, unlawful,

nihilist, indeed 'savage', because modernizing ideas about state and society eroded the traditional ties that kept life going despite the instability caused by independence and by the civil wars fought almost without interruption during the first half of the nineteenth century. Although Borges's family ties bound him to the modernizers among the elite, he also realized that traditional values were being threatened, and he was aware of the fragility of the abstract relations that modernity was establishing by means of material progress and republican institutions.

The search for a new social and political order was the main objective of the modernizing programme of the nineteenth century. But such an order could not be established merely through institutions: a new set of values had to be implanted in order to give stability to a fragile and loosely-knit society. Moreover, as we have noted, the arrival of thousands of immigrants in the last decades of the century, reinforced the sense of a new order, but an order with no fixities. At the beginning of the twentieth century, intellectuals began to consider the difficulties, not just the advantages, of being a new and young country. Because the transition to a modernized republic, governed by formal institutions, had proved painful and difficult, they could point to the solidity of traditional rural values. Although most of them praised the formal structure of modern Argentina, at the same time a sense of insecurity, which was not merely the result of a reactionary or elitist viewpoint, pervaded their images of society and their sense of the future. If few looked back to the past as a source or a model for the present, it was nevertheless seen as a time when society had had knowable dimensions and when values were shared, not as a result of formal pacts, but because they sprang from the same soil that nurtured common identities. Although the elite seemed satisfied with the modernization process (which opened up what appeared to be almost limitless economical opportunities), intellectuals found that the very process that had created modern Argentina was flawed by the absence of strong cultural bonds. Society was firmly entrenched, secularized and autonomous; but, as with all modern societies, its institutional and formal basis was deprived of the strong echoes of tradition and myth.

Borges stated this sense of loss (or absence) in one of his first essays: what Buenos Aires needed badly, he wrote, was ghosts. Although it could be read ironically, his assertion also implies a 'cultural politics': where the myths of a traditional society recede into an unretrievable past, the traces of those myths in literature construct an analogon not of a previous reality, but of an ideal model in terms of which a society can view itself. 'Ghosts' imply a common ground and a sense of harmony with the past. In a society where modern institutions founded on written law had eroded traditional beliefs and 'natural' bonds, the fact of sharing the same 'ghosts' opened up, symbolically, the possibility of retrieving the sort of deep cultural awareness threatened by a modern republic itself riven by conflict.

The question of how a social and cultural order is established, preserved or destroyed belongs to the philosophical dimensions of political theory, a dimension that is seldom mentioned in relation to Borges, whose fascination with philosophy, by contrast, has attracted almost universal critical attention. I would argue that political philosophy is present in a real sense in some of his very finest stories, for the historical reasons that have been stated above and for reasons connected with world developments in the twentieth century. Around the mid twenties, when Borges stated that Buenos Aires was in sore need of ghosts, and that it was his task to provide them, the world had already been shattered by the First World War, and Western countries had been compelled to recognize the Russian Revolution and the building of the Soviet republics. At the same time, fascism had established itself in Italy, and had pervaded populist movements in other parts of Europe, and democracy had given way to political forms (tainted by populism and a plebeian style of mass politics) that had not been envisaged in the pure republican ideals of the liberal intellectual elites. Books such as Karl Mannheim's *Ideology and Utopia* and Julien Benda's *La trahison de clercs*,[2] as well as Ortega y Gasset's essays on the massification of culture, are the signs of a period marked by menacing and swift changes that profoundly altered the role of the man of letters in modern societies. Borges never explicitly took sides in this debate, which was certainly not restricted to Argentina. In fact he always stated his aversion to literature that chose to be permeated by political ideologies. In his 'Preface to the First Edition' of *Doctor Brodie's Report*, written in 1970, he states once again:

> My stories, like those of the Thousand and One Nights, try to be entertaining or moving but not persuasive. Such an intention does not mean that I have shut myself up, according to Solomon's image, in an ivory tower. My political convictions are quite well known; I am a member of the Conservative Party — this in itself is a form of skepticism — and no one ever branded me a Communist, a nationalist, an anti-Semite, a follower of Billy

the Kid or of the dictator Rosas. I believe that some day we will deserve not to have governments. I have never kept my opinions hidden, not even in trying times, but neither have I ever allowed them to find their way into my literary work, except one when I was buoyed up in exultation over the Six-Day War. The art of writing is mysterious; the opinions we hold are ephemeral, and I prefer the Platonic idea of the Muse to that of Poe, who reasoned, or feigned to reason, that the writing of a poem is an act of the intelligence.[3]

Yet the dramatic shifts in this century, like the rise of fascism, especially in Germany and Central Europe, left very visible traces in his fictions. Let us begin with the most explicit: racism is seen as an arbitrary form of state ideology that dismisses reason and distributes death at random, as in the case of Jaromir Hladik the writer–victim on whom God bestows 'the secret miracle'. Antisemitism as an obtuse ideology (which for Borges is, of course, a heavy indictment) is also examined in a famous dialogue in 'Death and the Compass'. When Inspector Treviranus discusses the murder of Doctor Marcel Yarmolinsky with Lönnrot, the 'pure reasoner', in the presence of the editor of the *Yidische Zaitung*, Treviranus dismisses 'rabbinical explanations' as useless. He immediately receives the sharp response of an enlightened *idéologue*:

> 'I'm a poor Christian,' he said. 'Carry off those musty volumes if you want; I don't have any time to waste on Jewish superstitions.'
>
> 'Maybe the crime belongs to the history of Jewish superstitions,' murmured Lönnrot.
>
> 'Like Christianity,' the editor of the *Yidische Zaitung* ventured to add.[4]

But there is also the much more complex case of 'Deutsches Requiem', a story built on the very explicit Nietzschean topic of violence prevailing over Christian virtues. A characteristically Borgesian critique of violence is offered from the standpoint of a German officer. By taking responsibility for the death of a Jewish poet, the officer hopes to destroy in himself every trace of compassion with regard to the Other and to what is different: Nazism is 'an act of morality, a purging of corrupted humanity'.[5]

The internal perspective Borges adopts in this story allows the argument of the Nazi officer to develop with its own logic; it emphasizes his options and his values, as the basis of an alternative order. Thus Borges makes the reader give him careful consideration instead of dismissing him out of hand. On the eve of his execution the German officer Otto Dietrich zur Linde, well read in Schopenhauer, Spengler and Nietzsche asks how human actions can be judged when they have been carried out to establish an order that entails a new organization of society along new principles. They can of course be judged from a moral standpoint which, if it is different from the one upheld by the founders of a new order, could be said to endorse evil instead of good. But, if viewed outside its historical context, the question of order is present in those systems which we approve as well as in those which we condemn. By offering a Nazi officer (the image of Ernst Jünger comes to mind in this portrayal of Otto zur Linde) as the voice of his story, Borges is pointing out the dilemma of all political orders, not only those that have been universally condemned but also those that we consider legitimate. Both offer arguments that might be logically developed. In fact, he is obliquely persuading us to reflect on the general question of order precisely because it is discussed by a 'civilized' and cultured Nazi who, as sub-director of a concentration camp, carried out the task of destroying the Jewish poet Albert Soergel. With the war over, Otto zur Linde asked himself why he felt relieved, and discarded several reasons before coming up with the truth:

> The world was dying of Judaism and from that sickness of Judaism, the faith of Jesus; we taught it violence and the faith of the sword. That sword is slaying us, and we are comparable to the wizard who fashioned a labyrinth and was then doomed to wander in it to the end of his days; or to David, who, judging an unknown man, condemns him to death, only to hear the revelation: *You are that man.* Many things will have to be destroyed in order to construct the New Order; now we know that Germany also was one of those things.[6]

A Borgesian theme runs through this passage: a man is himself and his enemy, fate runs its course through the blind consequences of our actions. Yet, there is something else here that cannot be overlooked. On the one hand, there is the organization of the world according to values, such as Nazism in the case of Germany. On the other, there is the idea that every order is based on the destruction of a previous one, based on different values, and that every order relies on an act of forceful imposition, although myths and philosophy can explain that imposition as a gift, a tradition, or a pact. Furthermore, the voice of the Nazi officer and his hideous racism put in question the naive belief that to demonstrate the validity and universality of values is a simple and straightforward intellectual exercise. Otto zur Linde is testifying not only to the extremes of Nazism, but also to the painstaking task of establishing our beliefs about what is right and wrong in society. 'Deutsches Requiem' chooses the difficult route of tackling this through the voice of a man almost universally condemned, and it explores at the same time the cruelty of even one death, that of a Jewish poet, and the dilemma of how a new order can be established. Society is constructed through violence, although the degree of violence and the values which legitimate it are, and should be, differentiated.

Questions concerning the foundations or the lack of foundations of values are related to questions about society. What is it that makes the existence of a society possible? How can a balance be kept between different customs on the grounds of collective administration or on the grounds of public interest? How is the very concept of the 'public' constructed, and how is power given to some positions and denied to others? According to what principles, which are not just based on punishment and reward, do men obey the law? Borges, in the footsteps of Swift, asks these questions of the reader of 'Doctor Brodie's Report'.[7]

Brodie, a Scottish Presbyterian missionary who had worked for the faith in Africa and Brazil, wrote (and left among the pages of Lane's *Arabian Nights' Entertainments*) a report on the 'Mlch' people, whom he calls Yahoos because of 'their bestial nature', and because it is difficult to give an exact transcription of their real name, since their language contains no vowels. The Mlch bear the mark of their literary ancestors, and can thus be considered as a quotation. The Mlch are transformed by Doctor Brodie (via Swift) into his 'Yahoos', in the report the narrator of the story has found and transmits almost in its entirety. This *structure en abîme*, a device Borges often used, releases the fictional power of the double quotation from Brodie and from Gulliver and, at the same time, establishes the text in a tradition of travellers to distant lands who find elements that mirror, in allegorical or ironic fashion, their own societies.

Like Swift, Borges opens up a moral argument through Brodie's report. But, unlike Swift, he does not propose an explicit term of comparison between the 'Yahoos' of Brodie's report and another people: there are no noble Houyhnhnms in his story, and their absence leads to different conclusions. While Gulliver has, at last, found in an animal society the opportunity to present a utopia, Brodie is only able, in the last paragraph of his report, to offer a tolerant opinion of his 'Yahoos', from a truly relativistic point of view: 'After their fashion, they stand for civiliz-ation much as we ourselves do, in spite of our many transgressions.' What does this mean? Is it merely an ironic conclusion or is there also a veiled critique of the civilization that produced Doctor Brodie's missionary expeditions?

Brodie ends his report with the 'fervent prayer that the Government of Her Majesty will not ignore what this report makes bold to suggest'. This is indeed bold, after the description of the 'Yahoos' that the report gives and the comparison that it draws between their civilization and the one to which Brodie belongs. It seems that nothing prepares us for this final remark: Brodie has been piously shocked by the cannibal habits of the 'Yahoos' who devour their king's and witch-doctors' corpses, and by the naive promiscuity of their Queen, who offers herself to the missionary only to be turned down. What, then, is he suggesting to Her Majesty? The 'Yahoos' have a rudimentary language — and Brodie finds it impossible to make out discrete logical parts of speech — composed of monosyllabic words, the meaning of which is regulated by the context or by the pragmatic forms of enunciation. They cannot discriminate between nature and culture (they consider that the hut Doctor Brodie has built for himself is a tree and are seen to be incapable of even perceiving such complicated objects as a chair). They have no idea of history and of the past in the broadest sense (only the witch-doctors are able to remember in the evening what has happened that same morning), and they make obvious and indeterminate predictions about what they consider to be the future (approximately the next ten minutes). They are not burdened by the weight of events, like the crossing of the Red Sea by the Hebrews, which we include in a past that has a bearing on our present. They are ignorant of remote causality and are thus deprived of notions such as fatherhood (which has hindered their conversion to the Christian faith and their understanding of the Christian concept of divinity). They endow poetry with a very special status that deprives poets of the right to life, because the poetic act has the power of turning them into gods with whom nobody communicates and whom anyone is entitled to kill.

Yet when Doctor Brodie gets back in touch with a civilized man, who happens to be a Catholic missionary, he feels shocked by the habits he has practised throughout his life: eating in public, for instance, which the 'Yahoos' avoided as a taboo: 'At first I found it revolting to see him open his mouth without the slightest dissimulation and put into it pieces of food. I still covered my mouth with my hands, or averted my eyes.'[8] Back in his own country, Doctor Brodie does not feel as Gulliver felt after his return from the land of the Houyhnhnms, except in the fleeting impression he receives from seeing that people eat in company without embarrassment. His fate is not that of Gulliver, who for years could tolerate no physical human contact, much less the spectacle of his family consuming food in his presence. Furthermore, Brodie does not yearn for the perfect happiness Gulliver had experienced, and learned to enjoy, with the Houyhnhnms, but instead recalls the 'essential horror' of his days with the 'Yahoos'.

Nevertheless he begs Her Majesty not to ignore what his 'report makes bold to suggest' — namely, a relativistic vision of a 'Yahoo' civilization which no reader of the report would consider civilized. He summarizes what makes the 'Yahoos' not only the barbaric nation he has described, but also a tribe whose organization and beliefs entitle them to the privilege of being considered civilized in the same way as Europeans:

> They have institutions of their own; they enjoy a king; they employ language based upon abstract concepts; they believe, like the Hebrews and the Greeks, in the divine nature of poetry; and they surmise that the soul survives the death of the body. They also uphold the truth of punishments and rewards.[9]

Doctor Brodie's report has made an unexpected and spectacular turn. On reaching this point, Her Majesty would doubtless be surprised by the earnest defence, based on a flawless cultural relativism, of the 'Yahoos'. She might ask on what grounds this level comparison between European nations and the 'Yahoos' is founded. What do the 'Yahoos' have that gives them the right to be placed alongside the Christian nations? Or, putting it in the terms of the last words in the story: what *is* the report's bold suggestion?

Readers of the report may decipher the suggestion as Doctor Brodie might have hoped Her Majesty would. The 'Yahoos' have found answers to the major questions concerning order in society without having to solve internal conflicts like modern Christian nations. They live in a perfect relationship with nature. In fact, since they are not able to discriminate between nature and culture, they do not experience the pain of that separation (although it also produces our civilization, industry, art and progress). Free of notions like 'remote cause' and effect, they are also untroubled by philosophical and scientific preoccupations. Since their language is completely free of a set pattern of meanings they only use words that express general notions. This is a language in which the power of speech might be considered weak, but this weakness prevents them from opening up potential areas of conflict over topics such as government or religion. They entrust the witch-doctors with the power to choose their leaders but believe that the doctors do so on the basis of certain character traits in the man chosen, which prevents quarrels over power and dynastic wars. They have a system of justice which unlike our own is not based on proof and argument: verdicts are given without more ado after the allegation of the crime. This nation is primitive if compared to the Christian nations, but at the same time it has solved for ever (or, at least, until their present state leads the 'Yahoos' to extinction) the question of order in society. Brodie's description of the nation, in the narrator's transcription, is no doubt ironic in its content, but not in its themes. The main characteristics of human organization are presented as in a sort of very ambiguous dystopia. Readers hesitate (as Doctor Brodie does) as to whether it is fair to judge the 'Yahoo' nation as a dystopia, in view of the fact that the 'Yahoos' themselves do not hold that uncharitable opinion about their own private and public regimes.

The effect of the story is equivocal, because although Doctor Brodie has decided to judge the 'Yahoos' according to his values, he finds that they have achieved results that are, at least formally, and no matter how crudely, those of an organized nation. The tone of his description fluctuates between emphasis on differences and the final discovery of the general similarities. Something of this hesitation is conveyed in the last words of the story. He begs Her Majesty not only to allow them, as Christians, to carry out the seemingly impossible task of saving the souls of the 'Yahoos', but he also hopes that the 'suggestion' of his report should not pass unnoticed. This suggestion is enigmatic, but could be understood as the conclusion of an elliptical comparative study of the habits of the Yahoos and those of the Christian nation. Brodie points out, at the end of his report, that the 'Yahoos' stand 'for civilization much as we ourselves do, in spite of our many transgressions'. He also adds that the horror of the experience he has undergone has not diminished since his return to Scotland: living in Glasgow, he feels that the 'Yahoos' are still around him. This feeling is neither explained nor justified in terms of a memory of the time he spent with them. It could be read in this way, but it could also be read as the trace of 'Yahooism' in the daily life of a Christian nation. Without doubt the 'essential horror of his experience' is part of the past; but it is not as obvious that the sense of being surrounded by 'Yahoos' in the streets of Glasgow can be so directly explained as a vestige of memory. After his assertion, he feels constrained to add: 'Only too well do I know the Yahoos to be a barbarous nation', as if he had to respond to someone who had challenged what, in any event, he had not written. Doctor Brodie is presenting a report but also an argument: that of cultural relativism. He has given voice to his repulsion but, at the same time, he has offered a balanced summary of the basic institutions of civilization: government, religion, arts and language.

But earlier in the report, almost as an aide, Brodie has offered the hypothesis that the 'Yahoos' were once a more civilized nation whose present decadence should be explained not as primitivism but as degeneration. Their coarse language which is built around very general concepts allows them, nonetheless, to 'draw abstractions'. His hypothesis is also based on some old inscriptions he has found, that the tribe is no longer able to decipher. The 'Yahoos' can be thought of as *the future of the European nations*, and not only as their past, just as Tocqueville discovered in the United States not the infancy of that country but the future of Europe.

'Doctor Brodie's Report' offers an unsettling mixture of fictional reportage and philosophical commentary: political philosophy through narrative. Borges's concern with the question of order in society thus takes the form of a classical genre. The traces left by his productive reading of Swift are so clear that they refer us back to a tradition of philosophical travellers, while at the same time alerting us to Borges's own uses of that tradition. While Gulliver is unambiguous with respect to his Yahoos (because he has the virtuous Houyhnhnms as a point of comparison), Doctor Brodie gives a puzzling verdict on his: at the beginning of the report they are seen as belonging to a 'bestial' race and, at the end, as standing, in their own way, for 'civilization', because in spite of their nature they have succeeded in building an order, which amounts to solving a political question. As readers of the text, we are left unsatisfied by our own opinions of this people. Following the argument, we would expect to experience only relief at Doctor Brodie's return to his country, but, instead, a careful reader is faced (as Her Majesty would have been faced) with a comparison between 'Yahoos' and Christian nations. Readers of Swift can find peace and security in the moral lesson the Houyhnhnms teach Gulliver, but readers of Borges do not have the same consolation, because there are no noble horses in the land of his 'Yahoos'. Yet a lesson is being given in the report, about different types of civilizations and different types of order based on values that appear to those on the inside as absolute truths, but which careful observers, such as Doctor Brodie, may in the end show to be contingent and relative. The report also offers a warning, albeit ambiguous and almost smuggled into the narrative, about the danger that threatens civilized nations: the barbarism which resides within them, and which Brodie could have encountered in the streets of Glasgow.

I do not claim that this is the only possible interpretation of the fantastic stories we have considered in this and the last chapter. We have read them with a sharp eye on their poetic principles and we have found that basic philosophical questions repose within the perfect lucidity of the narrative. The quest for an impossibly perfect order and the certainty that all order has unknown and terrible consequences is embedded in the perfection of the plot itself.

Notes

1. 'Poema conjetural', *El otro, el mismo*, in *Obras completas*, Buenos Aires 1974, p. 867. Translated by Anthony Kerrigan as 'Conjectural Poem', in J.L. Borges, *A Personal Anthology*, New York 1967, pp. 192-3.

2. It is at least very probable that Borges read Benda's book, for Benda was considered a sort of intellectual guru by the *Sur* group, to which Borges belonged.

3. *Doctor Brodie's Report*, Harmondsworth 1976, pp. 11-12.

4. 'Death and the Compass', *Labyrinths*, London 1970, p. 108.

5. 'Deutsches Requiem', *Labyrinths*, p. 176.

6. Ibid., p. 178.

7. In *Doctor Brodie's Report*, pp. 91-100.

8. For these quotations, ibid., pp. 99-100.

9. Ibid., p. 100.

PART TWO

THE AVANT-GARDE, BUENOS AIRES AND MODERNITY

SEVEN

The Adventure of *Martín Fierro*: The Avant-Garde and *Criollismo*

Borges is closely linked to three literary magazines of the 1920s, *Prisma*, *Proa* and *Martín Fierro*,[1] which promoted avant-garde programmes and in so doing revealed the ideological and institutional limits of the avant-garde in Argentina. Of these three publications, *Martín Fierro* had the widest audience and the highest visibility: modernizing young intellectuals who began publishing in the 1920s were known as *Martinfierristas* by friend and foe alike.

With the appearance of *Martín Fierro* in February 1924, we witness a typically modern aesthetic 'break' — that of the avant-garde. The scandal that the journal courted in order to achieve an immediate and wide-ranging recognition, the freedom with which it criticized *modernista* writers and those of the generation of the Centenario,[2] the polemics with socially committed and humanitarian literature, the parodic tone adopted in satirizing earlier and contemporary literary trends, all these aspects make *Martín Fierro* a sounding-board which echoed the changes in the textual system and the institutional battles then being waged. At the same time, the review's orientation differed from that of European avant-gardes in ways which demonstrate its limitations but also its originality.

If the European avant-garde combined a radical aesthetics with moral insurrection and a 'passion for dangerous experimentation', what can be said to define the Argentine avant-garde in which Borges played such a leading role? In order to characterize the type of departure made by *Martín Fierro* and the *Martinfierristas*, and to explain the largely moderate tone of their interventions, we must examine the nature of the intellectual field in Argentina between 1900 and 1920. The intellectuals, and the artistic *cénacles* in vogue at the time of the Centenario, created the conditions for the gradual professionalization of the writer and established ideological and cultural practices that aspired to long-term hegemony. The young *Martinfierristas* were to do battle with them in a struggle to establish their own aesthetic and institutional supremacy.

One journal, *Nosotros*, founded in 1907, had become the most universally accepted periodical of the time.[3] It published over one hundred pages of text monthly and not only covered developments in Argentine literature and plastic arts but also offered extensive news sections from abroad and translations of foreign articles. The directors of *Nosotros*, Roberto Giusti and Alfredo Bianchi, were typical literary promoters in a period that witnessed little differentiation in the artistic field, due, precisely, to the field's small scale and lack of complexity. *Nosotros* was consequently an ideologically and aesthetically eclectic publication. The programme of the journal was to organize and dis-seminate artistic and intellectual production and it considered that it represented the whole of the intellectual field. The avant-garde sought to break this unity, to divide the public and to debate with the hallowed writers of the day.

Martín Fierro attempted to break with the institutions and practices of the pre-existing intellectual field, whose development had, in fact, created the necessary conditions for the development of the avant-garde itself. At the beginning of the 1920s, in the two or three years that preceded the appearance of the journals in which Borges and his fellow writers participated (*Prisma, Proa, Inicial, Martín Fierro*), the intellectual field, under the hegemony of *Nosotros*, appeared relatively unified. In these years, the unity of the field was considered a prerequisite for its consolidation and expansion. For that reason, the directors of *Nosotros* included younger writers in their pages. Proof of this can be found in the development, within *Nosotros*, of those writers who were to become the leaders or members of the Ultraist[4] or *Martinfierrista* avant-garde. In 1921, *Nosotros* published a declaration by Jorge Luis Borges, titled 'Ultraismo', which developed some of what would soon become the aesthetic tenets of the avant-garde, and included five or six poems. Almost a year later it published an unprefaced 'Ultraist Anthology' and throughout 1923, it also published clearly Ultraist poems by Eduardo González Lanuza and Córdova Iturburu (both of whom would immediately join the ranks of the *Martinfierristas*), and an article by Borges, 'Berkeley's Dilemma', which prefigured ideas that he would develop in subsequent decades. *Nosotros* published the first anthology of Argentine Ultraism, with poems by Borges, Sergio Piñero, Norah Lange and Eduardo González Lanuza (all of whom, a few months later, would become noisy and conspicuous members of the vanguard literary *guerrilla*). In December 1923, *Nosotros* published another article by Borges ('On Unamuno, the Poet'), and in March 1924 it reprinted a commentary by Díaz-Canedo, which had appeared in Spain, on Borges's book of poems, *Fervor de Buenos Aires*. This article is virtually the last demonstration of the harmony between the most institutionalized sector of the intellectual field and those who, almost immediately, would become the avant-garde. When another journal of young writers, *Inicial*, appeared in October 1923, *Nosotros* greeted it with a virulent attack. For their part, the *Martinfierristas* began to find their own place in the network of cultural institutions.

Creating an Environment

The appearance of avant-garde journals, in particular *Martín Fierro*, profoundly affected the formal and informal institutions of the intellectual field. From 1924 onwards the avant-garde disputed the structures of the literary canon by waging war on *Nosotros*, *modernismo* and the writers of the Centenario. In the opinion of *Martín Fierro*, *Nosotros* reproduced and even acted as agents for the official system and its aesthetic criteria.

In a series of articles, the editors of *Martín Fierro* set out a programme to change the ways in which, traditionally, a literary pantheon had been created in Argentina. The journal began to compete for literary recognition within these institutions and participated in the system of official prizes. It accepted the institutions as a mechanism for promoting young artists and explicitly recognized the state's legitimate right to intervene as a regulator and promoter of the arts. Even Presidents of the Republic who attempted to foster artistic development could be, according to the avant-garde, 'fair to both parties'. But the avant-garde did warn against the danger of a 'politics of the club'. Instead of supporting a movement for aesthetic and institutional change, the 'politics of the club' was based on conciliatory agents such as *Nosotros* —

that is, on figures that had held power in the previous decade. This official policy brought 'no benefit to the country', the editors of *Martín Fierro* announced. In this aspect of their programme, the *Martinfierristas* worked for a peaceful reform of cultural institutions rather than adopting a radical perspective as *refusés*, after the fashion of the European avant-gardes.

The moderate line of *Martín Fierro* (in particular of Evar Méndez, its editor-in-chief and the author or driving spirit behind these articles), was limited to denouncing the politics of the *cénacle*, and demanding that the state intervene to put an end to favouritism in the awarding of official prizes. By proposing that literary prizes should depend on the Ministry of Public Education, *Martín Fierro* subscribed to a line of thought already to be found in older writers that the journal was attempting to overthrow: the obligation of the state to offer economic protection to artists who could not hope, in a society like the Argentine and in a literary market where a middle-class public preferred the realist novel to innovative experimentation, to live from the proceeds of their work. This call for state patronage, which was caused to a large extent by the lack of differentiation in the intellectual field, coexisted in *Martín Fierro*, and in the avant-garde in general, with an elitist rejection of those products which the rapidly developing publishing industry offered to a broader and obviously less cultured audience.

As well as stressing the need for institutional support for the development of art and literature, *Martín Fierro* also argued that the state had certain obligations in the field of cultural promotion, in particular the obligation to restore the balance in favour of younger writers, as opposed to well-established figures such as the 'national bard', Leopoldo Lugones.[5] Although it adopted a generally conciliatory attitude to state power, the journal would pick out certain enemies, such as the *intendente* of the city of Buenos Aires (an inefficient and conservative representative of the state), or *Nosotros*, which provided many of the jury members for municipal prizes. The anti-bourgeois tension of the European avant-garde was converted, in Buenos Aires, into a more moderate opposition to aesthetic philistinism and to the lack of taste of the average bourgeois or state bureaucrat.

This moderate line was sustained by the editorial board of *Martín Fierro* from the first to the last issue. Evar Méndez described the function of the journal as being 'to form an environment and to awaken literary life'. What this meant in practice was that the review helped to change the intellectual field, produce a new type of public, create new attitudes in literary life and modify taste. It was a profound change but not a nihilistic break or an anarchic confrontation with the existing order.

When *Martín Fierro* defined its function, therefore, it did so in terms of 'founding' certain literary activities. Important among these was the foundation of publishing houses linked to *Martín Fierro* and to *Proa*, which published the vanguard writers and had an explicit programme: they would be exclusive, partisan and tendentious, uninterested in commerce, respectful of authors' rights and of all the norms of modern book marketing (street advertising, promotional prices, special discounts to booksellers and so on). In other words *Martín Fierro* marked the beginning of the end of the system which had operated in previous decades, under which authors paid for their own work to be published.

The editors of the magazine were clearly more moderate than some individual members of the group, among them Borges and Oliverio Girondo,[6] who proposed a more radical aesthetic break. This moderation was due not just to their own ideological limitations but also to the limitations of the intellectual field and of the wider society. Sexual and moral repression, apoliticism, the disciplined support of the nation and of the rights and duties of the state – all point to a vanguard so attached to traditional ideologies that it could not question the social order in any profound way. But if *Martín Fierro* did not criticize the family, the nation, authority or religion, it did decisively change literary mores. Ulyses Petit de Murat, one of the members of the group, recalled that '*Martín Fierro* had included women in its literary banquets and in its lectures. Literature at that time was dominated by men. Norah Lange was a cornerstone of these meetings. She gave speeches standing on a table'. In fact all the memoir accounts of these years by avant-garde writers are unanimous in pointing to these new relations among writers. Indeed, such new relationships seemed to demand more energy than writing itself. Leopoldo Marechal,[7] one the most conspicuous members of the group, records that 'the rest of my time I dedicated to "literary life" and all that that entailed, rather than to literary creation … the *Martín Fierro* movement was firmly rooted in life itself'.

Martín Fierro had its friends and allies – two in particular: Macedonio Fernández[8] (revered by Borges as a *grand vieux*) and Ricardo Güiraldes.[9] In order to make these writers visible it was necessary for the *Martinfierristas* to reform the Argentine literary system. Only a change in the view of what literature should be allowed them to rescue Güiraldes from his isolation and discover Macedonio Fernández. The publication of their texts is one of the clearest vanguard gestures of the periodical's history.

Literature as a Commodity

The avant-garde reformed the literary system, denied the traditions and the genealogy of the intellectual field (by constructing alternative genealogies), and divided the public. It discovered precursors who had been left out of the established canon. It made a marginal, like Macedonio Fernández, into the centre of its system. It affirmed that those who did not read literature in this way were aesthetically reactionary, unable to understand the phenomenon of the 'new'. Apollinaire published Sade, the *Martinfierristas* published Macedonio Fernández: two great marginals outside the institutions and unknown to the market and to the public. These marginals shared a common viewpoint: they were opposed to the logic and the morality of the market (for the avant-garde, the logic of the market, its only raison d'être, was profit).

The avant-garde saw itself as embodying an aesthetic 'truth' which, in its opposition was to the 'truth' of commerce, revealed the real conditions of production for the market. But their opposition was so intense precisely because the avant-garde itself was also, in some way, a product of the market. Only a system of production of symbolic goods that conceives of the public as having various levels, and gears itself to one of them, can allow the circulation, in opposition to itself, of texts which can be defined in however illusory a fashion as outside the market and free of its regulations. But this 'being outside', which defines a moment of the avant-garde, is a space of conflict. The avant-garde does not conceive of itself as an alternative space in the intellectual field, but rather as the only moral and aesthetically valid space. Its conflict with the 'culture industry' and with 'middlebrow' and 'lowbrow' culture is both aesthetic and ethical. But, it also has a wider social significance. The avant-garde is possible when both the intellectual field and the market for symbolic goods have reached a relatively generalized and widespread stage of development. That is to say, when the writer feels both the fascination and the competition of the market, rejects it as a canonical space, but secretly desires its judgement. Competition in the market and for the public is a modern form of aesthetic competition. The tension can be so great, or the vanguard can feel itself so weak, that the retreat from the market is one possible option for competing in this world. When the avant-garde denies the market, it divides the public while at the same time demanding for its texts a type of reading practised, in the first place, by the writers themselves: a reading among equals.

The Argentine avant-garde lived this tension with the market-place and with the public: it rejected the former and proclaimed the need to form a new type of reader. To this end, it sought to reform taste and create alternative ways into the literary market-place. Two axes — profit/ art and Argentine/immigrant — intersect in the *Martinfierrista* attitude to literature as commerce. To make money out of literature is an aspiration explicitly linked to the class origin of a writer. There were no exceptions to this rule for *Martín Fierro*.

The conflict of the Argentine avant-garde with the 'culture industry' is not simply a reflection of European ideologies. From around 1915, Buenos Aires had seen the growth and prosperity of a literature produced for middle and lower social sectors which had relatively high weekly circulation figures and was published at accessible prices. At the beginning of the 1920s, in addition to these weekly publications, which included serials and adventure novels, there appeared collections of cheap books which offered translations of European narrative and theatre. 1922 saw the publication of perhaps the most successful collection of all, significantly called 'Los Pensadores' (The Thinkers).[10] The avant-garde identified this collection with the 'social' literature, naturalistic realism and *lumpen* sentimentality cultivated by the writers of a literary group known as 'Boedo'. The group was named after a working-class district of Buenos Aires where some of the writers lived, and where the publishing-house Claridad, which published them, had its offices.

In its rejection of the market, *Martín Fierro* condemned the profit motive (a reproach which could be applied to the publishers of sentimental serials and adventure stories) and decried 'edifying' literature, which it linked aesthetically to social realism, whose reading public belonged to the lower-middle-class and poorer social strata. If the development of a market for literary works was due to an increasing reading public, then *Martín Fierro* was faced with the problem of how to divide this public. There were important areas of Argentine literary production in the 1920s that the periodical chose to ignore, because they were linked too openly with the market and, by extension, with a public whose allegedly philistine taste the avant-garde repudiated. If the goal was to create a new public (and this was *Martín Fierro's* explicit programme), then the established taste of the market-place had to be destroyed. Literature published in thousands of copies, in cheap and often shoddy editions, seemed to the journal to be a corrupt form of competition. Hence the elitist criticism of the writers of the Boedo group, to the effect that, their appeal to social literature notwithstanding, they had their eye on the market.

This contrast between profit and art in the intellectual field thus has a wider social significance. The ethical tone that *Martín Fierro* adopts when it talks about success in the market-place, a tone which cannot be seen as purely dishonest, as a mere ideological representation or as a symbolic denial, is overlaid by class: 'We know', reads an editorial in *Martín Fierro*, 'of the existence of a subliterature which feeds the unscrupulous greed of commercial companies created to satisfy the low taste of a semiliterate public.' The link between the commercial nature of popular publishing and the 'inferior' sensibility of its readers is also a clear comment on the origins of the writer and the money that literature can produce. In these circumstances, the *Martinfierristas* proclaimed the truth of the avant-garde which condemned the commercialization of art.

The poetics of 'social' literature were, therefore, not only defined by its 'left-wing' or 'humanitarian' ideology, but also by the demands of the market and the social origins of its writers. With regard to the writers themselves, *Martín Fierro* was at its most implacable. This literature was supposedly written with a characteristic 'deformation of pronunciation' which revealed its immigrant origins. The journal once more hauled out the theme of linguistic purity as the hallmark of Argentines with old Hispanic-criollo ancestry. The notion of 'linguistic purity' had pre-occupied some of the writers of the Centenario, whom *Martín Fierro* considered enemies. Yet the journal shared their views in its satires of the 'uncouth jargon infested by Italianisms' thrown up by a literature which wallowed in 'slum stories' written by 'Italo-criollo' writers. There were therefore two types of writer and two publics: those who were 'Argentines without effort', because they did not need to disguise a foreign accent, and those who by their origin and their language could not claim to be part of any long national tradition.

The angry violence of this attack (which was not typical of the generally parodic and humorous tone of the journal) illustrates the fact that what is being debated is a fundamental question from both an ideological and an aesthetic point of view. The debate between profit and art was overlaid by the social contradiction between old Argentines and immigrants. This can be seen in the acknowledgement that *Martín Fierro* gave to the first edition of *Proa*, the other great journal of the avant-garde: much could be expected of the members of this group, it argued, since they were 'deeply rooted in tradition, and their surnames show them to be from families that are Argentine through and through'.

Class origins, the relationship to national tradition, the purity or corruption of language, the attitude towards the literary market: all these elements make up a 'structure of feeling' shared by the Argentine avant-garde to which Borges belonged. Not all the elements of this structure, or the literary forms that expressed it, have the same weight. The very dynamic of the avant-garde on occasions eroded the importance given to cultural tradition and the nation. However, the control over language and the relationship with the 'low-class' public are constantly stressed. This lowbrow public, from which the avant-garde kept its distance, contaminated language, imposed a 'deformed' pronunciation and helped to foster an 'illegitimate' use of the *conventillo* in realist literature. (We shall see shortly how the *conventillo* could have a 'legitimate' use in literature.) The public that the avant-garde approved of were those who turned their back on the market. Defined by their sensibility towards the new, this public was opposed in more than one way to the public that read the realist works of the Boedo group. In social terms, the Boedo public was from the surburban neighbourhoods and not from the centre of the city. These were readers who were unsure of their Argentine language. Aesthetically, their tastes ran in the main to short stories and novels, whereas the *Martín Fierro* public read poetry and essays. Here we have two publics and two literary systems, two systems of translating foreign literature and two groups each of which accused the other of cosmopolitanism.

The Avant-Garde and *Criollismo*

The name that the most important avant-garde magazine adopted, *Martín Fierro*, needs to be considered. The question is an important one, for the name itself alludes to a central theme, that of nationality.

Why is the question of cultural nationalism so persistent in

Argentina? Around 1910 writers as prestigious as Ricardo Rojas and Leopoldo Lugones reinterpreted the gauchesque poem *Martín Fierro*, written by José Hernández in the last third of the nineteenth century, as a culmination and synthesis of national values. The background to this insistence is the presence, first, of intellectuals from outside the traditional upper classes who are part of a general process of growth of the middle sectors, and, secondly, of urban popular sectors of immigrant origin. For the first time the question of national identity is posed in a systematic and dramatic way, the reason being the presence of thousands of immigrants in a country which needed them as a labour force but feared them as a political and cultural force. Nationalist writers offered two different solutions: some like Ricardo Rojas, proposed a fusion of the native population, be they Spanish, criollo or indigenous, with the immigrants and their offspring; others, like Leopoldo Lugones, saw a threat to Argentine culture in the linguistic, racial and ideological pressures exacted by the new arrivals.

In these terms, at least, the debate was not resolved in the 1920s. The editor of *Inicial*, one of the modernizing journals of the period, claimed that it was only in the 1920s that intellectuals began to debate the question of the nation. This remark, which is historically false, since obviously the writers of the Centenario conducted similar debates before the 1920s, nevertheless reveals an ideological truth. For the avant-garde the inconclusive debates about national culture became another key issue to be resolved as part of a vast movement of aesthetic renovation. The first issue of *Martín Fierro* announced its appearance under the slogan, 'The Return of Martín Fierro'. This phrase carried a heavy symbolic charge, based as it was on a gaucho hero who was perceived as a 'national essence', which the avant-garde could once again embody. This insistence on the essence of Argentina (*Argentinidad*) was apparently a necessary precondition for the magazine's carrying out its mandate for change. The decision to support a programme of nationalist cultural regeneration is another of the contradictions that run through the history of the magazine. In the 'Manifesto' that was published in issue 4, cultural tradition is described as a 'family album' which cannot be denied, but which cannot at the same time be held up for fetishistic veneration. However, in the same 'Manifesto', one aspect of this national question is highlighted as one of the new features of the avant-garde: linguistic nationalism, as expressed in the phrase '*Martín Fierro* has faith in our phonetics'.

In its polemic with the social-realist literature of the Boedo writers, one of the main theses of *Martín Fierro* is the difference, in literary terms, between 'Argentines without effort' (members of the Hispano-criollo tradition) and the sons of immigrants. The key to this difference lies in the relationship that each group has with the language, in particular with spoken language and its phonetic variations. *Martín Fierro* describes the literature of Boedo as being produced by those who have an external relationship with Spanish and therefore need to disguise their foreign pronunciation. Closeness to oral language and its 'natural' acquisition was seen as a condition and a guarantee of Argentine writing. Any relationship with language based on the repression of a foreign language (brought in by the immigrants) would produce a literature marked by the spurious origins of the writer. It was assumed, of course, that the 'bad' foreign languages were those spoken by immigrants, since there were also 'good' foreign languages — those that the Hispano-criollo Argentines learned through culture and literature.

In the discourse of *Martín Fierro*, nationality is taken as a given. But how could this 'national essence' become the stuff of literature? In his review of Borges's book of poetry *Luna de enfrente*,[11] Leopoldo Marechal points to rhetoric as being an obstacle to language as spoken and heard: Borges writes his poetry 'in a language beloved to us, because it is the language that we truly speak, unencumbered by the frills of rhetoric.' Oliverio Girondo also considers that linguistic identity is a given and that due to its immediacy it cannot be gained through 'intellectual effort' or any other work that language acquisition presupposes. The question of social origins (which was seen as so closely tied to the profit motive or to a lack of interest in art) was considered decisive with regard to language. Once again these literary conflicts duplicated and deformed the conflicts of another system: the difference between old Argentines (i.e. sons of traditional families, who bore creole or European surnames established in Argentina for decades) and *gringos* (who had unknown surnames) was re-enacted in the debates of the avant-garde.

This insistence on the nuances and variations of oral language can be seen as part of a longstanding debate over the nature of language in Argentina: the special features of the Spanish spoken on the River Plate. From the first Romantic generation of writers onwards, we find a constant defence of the right of Argentine intellectuals to renovate language and combat any hegemonic pretensions of Spanish as spoken in Spain. This theme of linguistic independence was coupled in *Martín*

Fierro, as in the Romantics, with a declaration of the right to 'contaminate' literary language with socially and culturally prestigious foreign languages. The ideal of Gallicized Spanish as the only possible language for Argentines, which Sarmiento defended, the nineteenth-century ideal of the polyglot, reappeared in a caustic response by *Martín Fierro* to *La Gaceta Literaria* of Madrid. *La Gaceta* had suggested that, in order to combat the supposed danger of linguistic fragmentation in Hispanic America, Madrid should become the region's 'intellectual meridian'. Borges scorned this pretension to literary purity by ironically pointing out that 'Madrid is a city whose only intellectual invention is the Gallicism — at least, in no other part do people speak so much about it'. Borges's implication was that although the Spaniards accused the Argentines of speaking a deformed, Gallicized Spanish, their own linguistic purity was a mark of their obtuseness: they talked a lot about Gallicisms, but did not have the wit or intelligence to use Gallicisms productively.

The discourse of *Martín Fierro* answers the question as to which people, by their 'natural' relationship with language, can be polyglots. An Argentine polyglot is someone who has the Spanish of the River Plate as a mother tongue: only on the secure basis of these origins can a legitimate polyglotism be constructed. One can read, translate, and even write in French or English, but one's pronunciation of Spanish decides everything. Only through phonetics, which in the words of Oliverio Girondo should be as natural as 'lacing up our boots', could one gamble with, and win control over, language.

The language question is one chapter in a vast and, for Argentine intellectuals, obsessive debate over cultural tradition. In the first literary questionnaire organized by *Martín Fierro*, the definition of a 'national' was given as one who had an 'Argentine sensibility and mentality'. The question of cultural nationalism, and by extension of cosmopolitanism, divided the intellectual field along distinct class lines. The social writers of the Boedo group rarely brought the matter up; when they did, it was to accuse the avant-garde of being truly *extranjerizante* (following foreign models in an unquestioning fashion). The members of *Martín Fierro*, as well as declaring themselves to be heirs of this 'natural' cultural identity, threw the argument back at Boedo, accusing them of being linguistically and culturally foreign.

In fact, the question of cosmopolitanism should be read as a definition of different positions in a disputed intellectual field: the cosmopolitan is always the other. And in the case of the 1920s avant-garde, cosmopolitans are those who translate books other than those translated and read by the writers of *Martín Fierro*.

The Tradition of the Avant-Garde

In issue 22 of *Martín Fierro* there appeared a note signed by Oliverio Girondo arguing that a campaign to erect a monument to José Hernández should receive 'the support of every artist without distinction'. The editors of the magazine took up this suggestion with enthusiasm and expanded the argument by setting out the main lines of a tradition of writers who 'have the deepest national roots and in whose work future Argentines will search for, and discover, their spirit and origin'. The names which should make up this tradition were discussed on several occasions. (Borges, for example, suggested Eduardo Wilde, a short-story writer and politician of the last third of the nineteenth century.)

But one important link in this tradition, *criollismo*, appears as its ideological and aesthetic centre. The question of *criollismo* is a constant theme in *Martín Fierro*. There is legitimate *criollismo* and false *criollismo*, a necessary *criollismo* and an 'exaggerated' *criollismo*, superfluous from the point of view of literary language or of plot. It is almost a national Argentine tradition for *criollismo* to become the centre of a dispute and for one form of *criollismo* to be supported explicitly against another form. Sergio Piñero, in a bibliographical review of Borges's *Inquisiciones*,[12] outlines the question in terms similar to those used by Borges himself some years later: 'I think it unnecessary to refer to the lasso, to the rodeo or to stallions as though they were, or as though they manifested, the soul of the gaucho'. The question asked by the *Martinfierrista* is what can guarantee a 'true localism', and, by extension, who can write a literature in which *criollismo* is not seen simply as picturesque or full of local colour.

The avant-garde thought that it could 'purify' *criollismo* of these excesses and, following Borges's lead, invent a new space: urban rather than rural *criollismo*, *criollismo* that set in the *orillas*, on the outskirts of the city, the neighbourhoods far from the centre, with its houses and vast patios, its stores, and the fleeting presence of the *compadrito* in the door of the tenements. Borges outlined this aesthetic programme in his first three books of poems[13] and in the short story 'Hombres pelearon' (Men Fought), which *Martín Fierro* published in 1927.

The Aesthetic Principles of *Martín Fierro*

Over forty years after the end of the *Martinfierrista* moment, some members of the group agreed that the journal had offered a space for an eclectic avant-garde. '*Martín Fierro* was a sort of cocktail of the new generation. There was not much selectivity. All tendencies were represented, but the dominant mood was one of superficial aggression.' Such was the view of Brandán Caraffa, who had also edited *Inicial*. Another participant, the nationalist historian and translator of Virginia Woolf, Ernesto Palacio, added, 'It was like that until Ricardo Güiraldes and Oliverio Girondo joined: it was something ambiguous, without many objectives. It was these two writers who brought with them the ferment of literary renovation and made the quest more systematic'. Leopoldo Marechal recalled that there was no unifying aesthetic but rather 'a desire for renovation, a need to update our literature and art'.

The different strands of the Argentine avant-garde, however, shared a common enemy: Lugones and the lackeys of *modernismo* were unanimously rejected. The poetics of *modernismo* were in effect banished to the basement of Argentine letters by the *Martinfierristas*. In the manifesto of *Prisma*, written by Borges in 1921, the literary enemy was described as 'the blue tattoo of Rubén Darío', as 'ornamental junk' and as 'garrulous anecdotalism'. All this against a literature which had been revolutionary when Rubén Darío inaugurated the movement in the last two decades of the nineteenth century.

The theoretical poverty of the magazine explains why criticism in *Martín Fierro* was always more primitive than its literary texts. It was a magazine of poets, according to its own contributors, and only Borges and Macedonio Fernández showed that the avant-garde could possibly express itself in prose. Criticism of books reiterated the tenets of the avant-garde – that the public should finally understand and accept modern art, that they should reform their taste, recognize true values and adopt a 'new sensibility' – all in a friendly dithyrambic style characteristic of the journals that *Martín Fierro* abused.

But the journal made one obstinate claim for itself: that it alone was the aesthetic left-wing of the intellectual field, the most revolutionary sector of Argentine literature. This place was disputed by social writers who declared themselves to be on the left of the political spectrum, but *Martín Fierro* dismissed them as literary reactionaries, linked to European groups such as the journal *Clarté*, directed by Henri Barbusse, who were described as presenting 'the worst aesthetic manifestations of reaction'.

Boedo was placed firmly on the aesthetic right since it adopted a programme of naturalism, which became ultranaturalism 'in its most crude and sordid aspects, trying to stir up in the reader not simple emotion, but horror and disgust'. *Martín Fierro* used the argument that such writing belonged to an 'aesthetic of the archive': naturalism, because of its objectivity, became totally unfeeling. The new literature, by contrast, 'should gut the dummies of naturalism, and delve into the entrails of all those characters that writers of naturalism offer us in such a superficial way'. The new literature contrasts an 'aesthetic of reproduction' with an 'aesthetic of sensibility'. But the magazine did not present any textual criticism or programme which could really be deemed a radical alternative. In the face of ultranationalist literature *Martín Fierro* offered only one exceptional text, 'Leyenda policial' (Police Story) by Jorge Luis Borges, a 'proto-text' of 'Hombre de la esquina rosada' ('Street-corner Man').

Moderate Heroes

The hero of the Argentine avant-garde was a Spaniard: the Ultraist writer Ramón Gómez de la Serna. The *greguería*, a sort of aphorism based on a metaphor, which had been invented by him, was used productively by the *Martinfierristas*, and Gómez de la Serna was promoted by the two major poets of the magazine, Borges and Oliverio Girondo. In issue 14, Borges published an article entitled 'Ramón and Pombo'* in which he compared Gómez de la Serna to different texts and authors. First, to Walt Whitman: 'In Whitman, as in Gómez de la Serna, we see all of life. Whitman also expressed a miraculous gratitude for the scale, the tangible nature and the varied colours of things. But Walt's gratitude was satisfied in his enumeration of objects which make up the world, whilst the Spaniard's gratitude is expressed in a series of merry and passionate

---

*Pombo was one of the nicknames of Gómez de la Serna.

commentaries on the singularity of each object.' It is significant that it was Borges who drew this comparison: in effect he is proposing his own way of reading. For Borges, Gómez de la Serna is insufficient, albeit admirable, as a writer until he is taken out of his own context and placed in a new network of readings which include Whitman but also the *Celestina*, Rabelais, and Burton's *Anatomy of Melancholy*. Borges also provided the most sophisticated readings of European writers, in a journal that rather predictably published Apollinaire, Valéry Larbaud, Supervielle and Giraudoux.

In fact a significant characteristic of *Martín Fierro* was its neglect of the most radical European avant-garde movements. They translated Paul Eluard for the first time when the magazine was about to close, in 1928. Surrealism, whose first manifesto appeared in the same year that *Martín Fierro* was founded, received only cursory mention in a few notes and in a very condescending article on Soupault. Along with Ultraism and Gómez de la Serna, the real leader of the avant-garde, to judge by the space given to him in the magazine, was Marinetti, who was greeted as a 'great man of action and thought'. Borges never shared this view.

The moderate nature of the Argentine avant-garde is responsible for these attitudes. Ideological barriers prevented it from becoming radicalized and imposed several *idées fixes* which were equally moderate. In the first place, these avant-gardists rejected any form of nihilism. Opposition to nihilism was presented in different ways in several key texts. It was necessary, they argued, to work for 'the new', but 'there was no sense in enlisting in the ranks of the iconoclasts'. Thus, the young literati, it was argued, should seek to dislodge preceding generations but they also had a duty to put in place 'new ideals'. Secondly, this avant-garde was concerned to establish a national genealogy in the field of culture, an agenda which allowed them ferociously to attack some *modernistas*, but which also obliged them to accept the idea of cultural continuity. Finally, this moderate attitude led to their criticism of bourgeois philistinism being couched in exclusively aesthetic terms: they left untouched the moral philistinism, social hypocrisy and sexual, moral and ideological repression of their society. This *bien-pensant* attitude was clearly also linked to the ideological limits of Argentine society and the place of the intellectual elite within that society. *Martín Fierro* was a modestly radical avant-garde because it did not take up a radical position with respect to social institutions and mores. Its programme — the creation of a literary environment and the reform of sensibility — did not affect the very conditions of existence of the intellectual.

This moderation is seen in their readings of the European avant-gardes and in the system that they constructed from these readings. It is tempting to compare this reading with that made in the same years by the Peruvian Marxist José Carlos Mariátegui. If Marinetti and Gómez de la Serna were the heroes of the Argentine avant-garde, Mariátegui thought of futurism as 'the so-called avant-garde which was saturated by conservative and provincial elements'. And surrealism, which, as we have seen, was practically ignored by *Martín Fierro*, was considered by Mariátegui to be the avant-garde par excellence, both tragic and desperate. The Argentines in this way shared with Spanish Ultraism its mistrust of, and remoteness from, historic vanguard movements.

Synthesis and Tensions

Yet in *Martín Fierro* a literary formula was developed, with its own original combination of elements, which was distinct from Ultraism even it if mirrored certain aspects of that movement. This formula was expressed in the texts of Borges, but it can also be read in Girondo, and traces of it can be found in certain key articles that are not signed. Here two legacies are fused: that of Gómez de la Serna and that of Evaristo Carriego (the minor, popular, local poet to whom Borges would later dedicate a book). This fusion is found even in the homages that *Martín Fierro* paid to certain writers. Issue 17 offers a homage to Carriego, issue 19 one to Gómez de la Serna. In his article 'Concerning Ramón's Arrival', Borges illustrates this synthesis.

> Carriego discovered the *conventillos* (tenements). Bartolomé Galindez, el Rosedal and I discovered the street corners of Palermo at sunset. Lanuza, all the birds.... The entirety of America, however, is still to be discovered, and the discoverer, now, is Ramón.... We will know everything through him. Through him we will know that the great Southern Cross is nothing more than a poor wake in the *barrios* (he will tell you of the miracle that your girlfriend will have seen for having such beautiful eyes).... Through him we will know that Yrigoyen will become President again because he is involved with not just the people but also the things of Buenos Aires. All this and much more Ramón will reveal to us; Rámon the man of the radiographic and tyrannical eyes which can only be compared to the eyes of that other conqueror of this America: don Juan Manuel de Rosas.

Similarly, in a review that Borges wrote of Oliverio Girondo's *Calcomanías* (Decalcomania), we find these two influences coming together once again, and today we can see that this was the real contribution of the avant-garde to Argentine literature. The fact that Borges put forward this premise more systematically than the rest is due to the density of his system of readings. Ultraism and Walt Whitman, but also Bishop Berkeley and the *Thousand and One Nights*: these are points of reference which distance him partly, but not completely, from the conventional system of the avant-garde. Other obvious points are his discovery of Macedonio Fernández and his early literary creation of Argentine myths.

But the coexistence in *Martín Fierro* of elements of different origins also reveals a tension which distorts many of its texts. This tension can also be seen between the contributors to the magazine: on one side were the editors, in particular Evar Méndez, while on the other were Borges, Oliverio Girondo and Macedonio Fernández. The *Martinfierrista* discourse was heterogeneous, based on a set of oppositions and vacillations that were never resolved. One tension links the name of the magazine, a hero of traditional gauchesque poetry, with a programme of aesthetic renovation: cultural nationalism *and* the avant-garde. The heterogeneous proposals that make up this programme might have given the magazine its originality, but they also set up a series of unresolvable contradictions. On the one hand there was the national subject, the gaucho Martín Fierro, on the other the European and cosmopolitan tenets of aesthetic renovation. It is certainly true that one part of Borges's work was concerned with resolving these contradictions. He ultimately overcame the tensions present in *Martín Fierro* by producing a body of work that might be defined as 'avant-garde urban *criollismo*'.

An affirmation of the new coupled with an adherence to a pre-existing cultural tradition; a campaign for what is 'characteristically Argentine', coupled with a cosmopolitan point of view: these are the elements that make up the ideological-aesthetic mélange of the avant-garde in the 1920s. The tension between *criollismo* and modernity or nationalism and cosmopolitanism might almost be seen as a constant in twentieth-century Argentine culture. All the great debates were organized around these tensions and the contradictions can still be found in the major texts of contemporary literature.

Notes

1. *Prisma* published two issues, in December 1921 and March 1922. The journal took the form of a poster which was displayed on the walls of Buenos Aires. It included some poems by Borges. *Proa*, whose editors included Borges and Ricardo Güiraldes, appeared between 1924 and 1926 (issues 1 to 15). *Martín Fierro*, the most successful and also the most irreverent of the avant-garde magazines, published forty-five issues between February 1924 and November 1927.

2. The 'generation of the Centenario' was a group of writers who came to prominence around 1910, the Centenary of Argentine independence from the Spanish Crown. Among these was the essayist Ricardo Rojas, who wrote the first history of Argentine literature, and the members of the magazine *Nosotros*, which helped to modernize the cultural field.

3. Founded in 1907 by Roberto Giusti and Alfredo Bianchi, *Nosotros* described itself as a 'monthly publication of letters, arts, history, philosophy and social sciences'. It published three hundred issues, the last of which appeared in December 1934.

4. The Ultraist movement was led in Spain, from the 1920s, by Ramón Gómez de La Serna. Its programme affirmed the image as the fundamental element in poetry, the abolition of logical and syntactical links, and the brevity of the poem as a formal proof of the condensation of meaning. Gómez de la Serna composed a special type of humorous aphorism, called the *greguería*, which transferred these poetic principles to prose.

5. Leopoldo Lugones (1874-1938) was the greatest Argentine *modernista* poet. Borges and the avant-garde writers felt obliged to debate with Lugones over poetic and aesthetic matters and they called into question his dominant influence over the culture of the period. It is important to remember that *modernismo*, in Latin America, is a movement that took place at the end of the nineteenth century, inspired by Parnassianism and French symbolism. It thus predates the avant-garde. On Leopoldo Lugones and *modernismo* in Argentina, see Chapter 3.

6. Oliverio Girondo (1891-1967) contributed to all the magazines of the Argentine avant-garde. His poetry, which was very different to that of Borges, dealt openly with themes drawn from the modern city and the changes in customs and daily life. In 1925 he published two books of poetry: *Veinte poemas para ser leídos en el tranvía* (Twenty Poems To Be Read on the Tram) and *Calcomanías* (Decalcomania) which had great success, mixed with scandal.

7. Leopoldo Marechal (1900-1970) was a poet and novelist. In his novel *Adán Buenosayres*, published in 1948, Marechal satirized the vanguard writers of the twenties and thirties, including Borges.

8. Macedonio Fernández (1874-1952) was the *grand vieux* of the Argentine avant-garde. Up to the 1920s, Macedonio, as he was known, had been a marginal and secret writer, but then his extremely original books began to be published alongside those of the younger writers. Fragmentary and eccentric, his work mixes fiction, essays and poetry with no respect for the traditional boundaries between genres. Borges's devotion to Macedonio is well known.

9. Ricardo Güiraldes (1886-1926) co-founded, with Borges, the magazine *Proa* and had been at the forefront of aesthetic modernization since before 1920. In his early books he attempted to overcome the aesthetics of *modernismo* and of Lugones. His most famous work, the novel *Don Segundo Sombra*, is a criollo Bildungsroman written from the standpoint of the new literary movements. Its immediate success compensated him for years of intellectual ostracism.

10. This collection included works by Gorky, Andreyev, Tolstoy, Lenin, and Bukharin.

11. Published in Buenos Aires in 1925.

12. A book of essays published in Buenos Aires in 1925.

13. *Fervor de Buenos Aires* (1923), *Luna de enfrente* (1925), *Cuaderno San Martín* (1929).

EIGHT

Utopia and the
Avant-Garde

The New as a Foundation

'Sweet yearning' does not delight our spirits and we would like to see all
things in their first flowering. And while wandering through this unique,
dazzling night, whose magnificent gods are the august reflections of golden
lights, like Solomonic genies, imprisoned in glass cups, we would like to feel
that everything in the night is new and that that moon which rises behind a
blue building is not that eternal circular arena over which the dead have
performed so many rhetorical exercises, but a new moon, virginal, aurorally
new.

Borges, 'On the Margins of the Modern Aesthetic'

Despite its fin-de-siècle style, this strange statement by Borges, published
in the Seville magazine *Grecia* in 1920, expresses some of the spirit of
renewal that would soon afterwards be reflected in the magazines *Prisma*,
Proa, and *Martín Fierro*. If every literary movement develops in relation to
an aesthetic and ideological context which legitimates it (for example
through tradition, nationality, the social, the notion of beauty as an
autonomous agency), the young writers made the 'new' the foundation
of their literature and of the opinions that they formed about their
predecessors and contemporaries.

The spirit of 'the new' was at the centre of the literary ideology, and
defined the aesthetic conjuncture, of the Argentine avant-garde. This
desire to be seen as different distanced it, as we have seen, not only from
Leopoldo Lugones and *modernismo*, or from realism, but also from the

structure and organization of intellectual institutions at the beginning of the 1920s. When Borges returned to Buenos Aires, when Girondo published *Veinte poemas para ser leídos en el tranvía* (*Twenty Poems To Be Read on the Tram*), the state of the cultural field could be summed up in the desperation of Güiraldes, whose books, based on symbolist aesthetics, had been completely ignored by the critics. The social elite (to which Güiraldes belonged) considered his work extravagant and tasteless. A rapid glance at *La Nación,* the most important daily paper of the period, reveals that the processes of cultural modernization, in particular in Argentina, receive only scant mention in its pages. The references to books and to art, which frequently appear, cannot be seen as a coherent critical discourse. They are, instead, short introductory notes which include quotations or entire poems from the books under discussion; *comptes-rendus* of exhibitions put on in Buenos Aires; commentaries on contemporary local or European culture, highlighting precisely those writers and groups that the avant-garde despised. It is in the cinema section that we find some comments which show an awareness of cultural renovation (references to Griffith and Pabst, articles on set design or on the relationship between cinema and politics). The same can be said of the notes on foreign theatre, which were written in the main by Lugné Poe and Zacconi. This extremely fragmented information is registered on long wave, which could pick up very few new voices from Europe.

Ten years later, Néstor Ibarra, a fellow-traveller of the young avantgarde writers, described this early period:

> Jorge Luis Borges returned to his country in 1921. What can I say about the state of poetry then? Nothing could be more neutral or sluggish, nothing could be closer to decadence and death. The great Lugones had already given, twelve years earlier, of his best. Enrique Banchs in 1911 had offered almost his final word in *La urna* (The Urn), which contains some of the strongest sonnets in our language: innovatory in its themes and eternal in its sensibility. Carriego was copied and diluted many times; the most famous name was that of the prolific and minor *sencillista** poet Fernández Moreno. But these values were either accepted or ignored, they were almost never questioned or discussed; poetry, and in general literature and art, was the most boring and incidental aspect of the life of the country.[1]

---

*The term *sencillista* refers to poetry which attempted to capture the tone of colloquial language and work with everyday themes as opposed to the exoticism of *modernismo*.

Ibarra, an intelligent reader of Borges and a gentle critic of Ultraism, described the problems faced by what he called 'the modern' in the Argentine cultural field. His account coincided with *Martín Fierro's* commentaries on cultural institutions, the system of literary prizes, commercial theatre and criticism in newspapers. The feeling of discontent covered several areas: the pre-eminence of writers who had reached the end of their creative potential around the time of the Centenario; the myopia of the critics who were not receptive to the new tendencies; the eclecticism of cultural journals, above all *Nosotros*; the way in which cultural institutions were organized; the reading habits and preferences of the public.

This spirit of renovation was expressed through a series of grievances and protests. The young writers attacked the positions held by the great writers of the turn of the century, the poetics they defended and the authority with which they were invested. And they attacked the style of the journals and daily newspapers which formed the tastes of the reading public. The aesthetic context described by Ibarra corresponds to the first quarter of this century. In opposition to this situation there emerged a somewhat diffuse but sufficiently powerful literary movement which caused an important change in the institutional framework, including the major daily papers.

It was necessary to break with the eclecticism of the magazine *Nosotros*, which had been published continually for some twenty years, and with *La Nación*. Intolerance and belligerence replaced the tolerance and conviviality that had hitherto characterized the relationship between intellectuals. The winds of change caused divisions and polemics: this was the style of the avant-garde, which marked it out as distinct from *Nosotros*. All the actors in the cultural field were forced to take up new positions, because their hegemony was being seriously questioned and because the growing prominence of avant-garde writers threatened to overthrow the established order: 'the new' came to reorganize the system of intellectual hierarchies. In 1930, Ibarra could single out *Martín Fierro* as the driving force behind this movement.

'Non-stop activity and chaos, daring and independence, with no system and no serenity, *Martín Fierro* will remain forever as a witness to a great literary period in Argentina.... Thanks to *Martín Fierro*, literature has greater autonomy, is held in higher regard, and operates in a field which is less ungrateful than before.[2]

When contemporaries talk of *Martínfierrismo*, they refer to a cluster of magazines of the period, best represented by *Martín Fierro*, since that magazine offered the most thorough expression of the avant-garde break. But Ibarra goes further, arguing that *Martín Fierro* completed the process of making the aesthetic sphere autonomous, a project that had begun with *modernismo*, but had not been concluded in the years of the first cultural nationalist debates, around 1910. It is interesting to note what values underpin this process of increasing autonomy. The avant-garde defended autonomy not merely in the name of beauty but more particularly in the name of 'the new': the new could settle the question of legitimacy. It was not a minor part of their programme, but rather its structuring principle. And because the new was intransigent, the avant-garde asserted a maximalist position.

The concept of the new was in itself sufficient to draw up the battle-lines in the intellectual field, but it was not the only aspect of the avant-garde's programme. As we saw in the last chapter, the national-criollo content of the avant-garde and its moral moderation distinguished it from other contemporary movements in Latin America. But nationalism, in this period, was filtered through the lens of 'the new'. Borges often debates the nature of acceptable and unacceptable *criollismo*, the way in which certain forms, in their adherence to local colour, are products of the past, while others, in their rejection of such 'localism', are formal-aesthetic inventions grounded in the new. For him good and bad *criollismo* can be differentiated according to aesthetic values.

'The new' is also a judgement on the public which the avant-garde deliberately divided, in contrast to magazines such as *Nosotros* which had always sought to homogenize and unify the reading public. *Martín Fierro* insulted the 'hippopotamic' and 'honourable' public, marking out for themselves an exclusive space far from the all-embracing *Nosotros*. The magazine *Poesía* published a letter from Macedonio Fernández to its editor, laying out an aesthetic of negativity, which was opposed to pleasure, and by extension opposed to the reading public.

> For this reason I give the name of 'culinary' to any art that makes use of sensory images just for the sake of pleasure itself and not as a means towards expressing certain emotions. Thus all versification is culinary in its rhythm, in its harmony, in its onomatopoeia and in the sonorous nature of its words and the rhythm of its accents.[3]

Macedonio Fernández clearly exposes those elements of the avant-garde programme which would lead to a fragmentation of the public. Whereas *modernismo* and the decadent movement had made great use of the sensory, the avant-garde sought to destroy it. Where *modernismo* had sought to increase readership, the avant-garde deliberately limited the field and saw comprehensibility as a negative value. These aesthetic strategies affected literary production and also the receptivity and the expectations of readers.

Alberto Hidalgo, a Peruvian poet who played an active part in the skirmishes of the Argentine avant-garde, set out, in a long text which appears as a prologue to his book of poetry *Simplismo*, a number of ways of reading which presuppose (or demand) a public prepared to engage with quite complex issues, in marked contrast to the 'spontaneity' of reading *modernista* and *postmodernista* works. Hidalgo developed a poetics of 'pauses', with a strong prescriptive element, since these pauses define the meaning of the poem rather more than the words themselves:

> In *Simplismo*, the pauses have an unexpected importance. The pauses become something like intervals. One cannot do without them in the reading if one wants to experience fully the poetic instant that flows from each verse independent of the global harmony of the poem. The pause is not a typographical expedient but rather a psychological state. At times it is more important than the line that precedes it.[4]

Let us imagine this reading public which is warned to keep away from a book because it does not contain cheap thrills; whose tastes are considered as part of a culinary, anti-artistic dimension of literature; who are told to mock Lugones, as Borges does brilliantly on numerous occasions; who are told how to read, and told that the blank spaces on a page are more significant than words: we are dealing, of course, with a *future public*, one yet to be constructed by means of one of the most successful operations of twentieth-century Argentine culture.

In this sense, the avant-garde was radical and optimistic. It did not share the social aspirations of humanitarian writers or those of the Left; its optimism was based on what Adorno called the 'historically ineluctable'. The Left envisaged a public that had to be educated, or heralded a public who could become readers through their own social development. 'If the workers cannot read us yet', argues Raúl González Tuñon, 'there are intellectuals, artists, journalists, painters, teachers and students who desire the transformation of society'.[5] Both these attitudes were attempts to establish left-wing intellectual foundations. The avant-garde shared the wish to oppose the philistines (a term often used by *Martín Fierro*), the *pompiers* and the traditionalists who wanted no art that did not wallow in feelings. But it hoped for new readers who shared the imagination of their chosen writers. The avant-garde of the 1920s was not interested in pedagogy: rather than educating, it sought to demonstrate, to issue proclamations, and to provoke.

For the avant-garde, 'the new' was located in the present; for the Left, 'the new' was a promise for the future. Thus their value systems were different: Whereas the Left thought that social transformations or revolution were the main pillars of their artistic practices, the avant-garde considered that it embodied new values that it could define and carry out. The pedagogic Left worked on the long view, while the radicalized Left placed itself in the orbit of the revolutionary cycle. The avant-garde was a utopia which transformed existing aesthetic relations: it offered the luminous and instantaneous establishment of the new.

This explains why the avant-garde was so actively engaged in transforming the cultural context, and why its tactics appeared so extreme. The avant-garde confronted the other fractions of the intellectual field and established what they considered to be a dividing-line between old and new. Hidalgo, Huidobro and Borges, in the prologues that they wrote for the *Indice de la nueva poesía americana* (Index of the New American Poetry, 1926), considered themselves to be on the other side of the line, at a zero-point in the history of poetry. Huidobro dedicated his prologue, in a characteristic pose that he repeated in each one of his manifestos, to a declaration of his own importance as an avant-garde creator. Borges declared *modernismo* to be dead and buried: 'Rubenism is exhausted, at last, thank God.' Hidalgo repeated the attack on *modernismo*, finding value only in José María Hidalgo, after whom 'nothing important happened until Huidobro appeared' as the founder of Ultraism. One year earlier, in the prologue to *Simplismo*, Hidalgo had offered his own periodization for the history of poetry. He established a 'troglodyte era' between Homer and Victor Hugo, which included Darío, followed by a break caused by Rimbaud, followed by the avant-garde which could be summed up, logically, in his own work. These delirious moments are an integral part of the foundational impulse of the avant-garde, and of the force and conviction of its programme with 'the new' at its centre.

The *Index of New American Poetry* must be read as a manifestation, under the guise of an anthology, of the avant-garde utopia: these are texts that change the aesthetic conjuncture. One could argue whether or not they are all part of a homogeneous programme. Perhaps not, despite the heavy-handed way in which Hidalgo dealt with those writers whom he excluded. Girondo, for example, is not included in the anthology, because Hidalgo declares that he has left out any imitators of Gómez de la Serna. Arbitrary and somewhat odd, the *Index* can be read as a statement of poetic art and also as the realization of a desire: the exclusions and inclusions together make up a literary map which establishes its legitimacy in the face of tradition, while trying at the same time to exclude this tradition. It changed literary relationships, promoted aesthetic principles and gave examples of what writing should be thenceforward. In the anthology there are writers who, in the words of Borges, must first carry out a work of destruction: 'Before beginning any explanation of the latest aesthetic, it is necessary to unmask the Daríoisms and anecdotalism of current literary practices which we, as Ultraist poets, seek to expose and abolish.'

The *Index* is also an expression of this avant-garde aesthetic in the emphasis it places on two complementary themes: urban modernity and the recuperation of a past or imagined Buenos Aires. Eduardo Gónzalez Lanuza developed the first of these themes not just in the title of the poems he included — 'Instantaneous', 'A Motor Car Poem', 'An Elevator Poem' (which Hidalgo also wrote about) — but also in the view he offered of the urban landscape. In 'There Are Distant Places Fifty Metres Away', the modern city is seen to alter the experience of space, in images that also occur in painting: 'dislocated landscapes/flee round the corners'. Space is modified because speed becomes a principle of the perceptive system and of representation. The same is true of noise, which did not appear in earlier poetry: 'words hang from the cables/ hooters, squealing, voices'. Jazz is a central theme: 'When the jazz-band of the angels/plays the fox trot of the Last Judgment ...'. A cubist decomposition of the urban continuum, the impact of modernity on the system and forms of perception, the destruction of the 'natural' contact between man and his surroundings, the construction of new images out of this amalgam of fragmentary allegories — all these are themes of the new poetry.

Another theme is that of the lost city, which the literature of the period, and especially the work of Borges, invents or reconstructs. Borges went báck to Buenos Aires bearing the good news of Ultraism; at the same time he was working with both literary and emotional aspects of the past. His poetry was part of an aesthetic, a sensibility and an urban landscape experiencing a rapid process of change. His system of perceptions and memories linked him to the past; his poetic project, on the other hand, was linked to 'the new'. He worked under the influences of aesthetic renewal and urban modernization to produce a mythology which contained premodern elements but which was filtered through aesthetic and theoretical avant-garde principles. In terms of topology, he brought the margins to the centre of the Argentine cultural system and established a new set of relations between the themes and the forms of poetry. He established the avant-garde usage of oral language in Argentina, a language that in these years was represented by the images of Ultraism. He established the centrality of the margins.

The poems printed in the *Index* demonstrate different avant-garde tendencies of the 1920s, not only because they use the rhetorical system of cubism and Ultraism, but also because, as a body of work, they show the force of the new ideologemes of urban modernization and aesthetic renewal at their most intransigent. But, unlike Huidobro or the Brazilians, the Argentine avant-garde did not place experimentation at the centre of its concerns. Its main intervention in the aesthetic field was the assertion of its *difference* to *modernismo*, and its originality is found in the blend of Ultraism and urban poetry.

The publication of the *Index of New American Poetry* was one of the main cultural confrontations of the twenties. The poems are the pragmatic demonstration of a conflict that could not be resolved through pragmatic means alone. The newness of the avant-garde (including its new version of *criollismo*) was outlined in successive programmes and manifestos. This explains Borges's incisive interventions in *Martín Fierro* and *Proa*, the aggressiveness of González Lanuza, the attacks by Leopoldo Marechal on rhyme and rhythms, the laments by Ricardo Güiraldes over his solitary past and his gentle friendship with the young writers, the cult status of Macedonio Fernández, the militancy of Oliverio Girondo and the vitality of Norah Lange.

In these years, as never before, Argentine writers produced many explanatory and polemical texts which, in the relative unanimity of their themes and outlook, can be seen as a programme of 'the new'. The main outlines of this programme can be found in Hidalgo, Macedonio, Borges, González Lanuza, and in the unsigned commentaries published by the little magazines. These are the years of attacks on the literary establishment: there are many discussions about the value system of the others, the old men, the followers of Lugones or Rubén Darío, the post-romantics. There is also an exposition of the value system of the new poetry.

The fractions of the intellectual field in this period articulated different ideas which would become the major concerns of later years: the 1930s developed the tendencies of the 1920s. Intellectual concerns were more complex and diverse than the relatively small number of issues that had been debated by the first cultural nationalist groups of the Centenario. From both an ideological and an aesthetic point of view, the writers established new literary foundations. On the question of cultural identity, which had so obsessed previous generations, the avant-garde groups considered that the concept of 'the new' was sufficiently powerful to assert its hegemony. At the same time however, and from the standpoint of the new, they gave voice to a different cultural nationalism. The great changes in culture in the period are related to changes in the foundations of the value system, that is to say, in the different answers to the question: 'What legitimizes a cultural practice, making it superior or preferable to other practices?'

In 1930, when Ibarra gave a fairly balanced and critical account of Ultraism (giving Borges a central role in this movement), he added a comment on the ideological-aesthetic blend that I have called 'avant-garde urban *criollismo*':

This artistic nationalism is, moreover, very modern — perhaps the only really modern aspect of our spirit.... This growing and organized intellectual nationalism is having a great influence on our young writers. The great apostle of *criollismo* is, as we know, Jorge Luis Borges. His *criollismo*, and he is the only writer to define it in a structured and non-verbose fashion, defines literary *criollismo* in general: neither Lugones nor Carlos de la Púa nor Jijena Sánchez can provide any argument or any work of art to counter him.[6]

This invention of Borges's brings an important aspect of 'the new' into play; it also offers a rereading of tradition made possible by Borges's blending of the avant-garde with a reassertion of the importance of foreign literatures.

But other definitions of 'the new' were circulating and being discussed in Buenos Aires. With the work of Huidobro, the avant-garde advanced an 'anti-content' position which affirmed the radical autonomy of art: the poet adds a dimension to the world which in any other way would have been unthinkable. Newness,as Huidobro never tired of repeating, was not to be found in the theme 'but in the way in which this theme is produced'.[7] Newness is formal, as Borges saw when he supported an aesthetic of refraction in place of an aesthetic of mimesis: 'There are, therefore, only two aesthetics: the passive aesthetic of mirrors and the active aesthetic of prisms.'[8] And Macedonio accepted only one valid definition of literature: 'The state of literary beauty should not contain (1) any instructive element or information (2) any sensory aspects (3) any aim other than itself.' Macedonio occupies the most extreme point in this discussion, due to his philosophical anti-naturalism, his idea that 'emotion' is a mental construct totally devoid of any notions of pleasure as an objective or as an end in itself.

Through such resistance to the positions of romantic and post-romantic poetry, the writing of poetry becomes a formal operation. The avant-garde was in this sense anti-psychological and anti-expressive. Borges put it as follows, anticipating his later construction of the poetic 'I' as a tissue of different voices:

> Lyric poetry has, until now, done nothing but oscillate between the search for auditory or visual effects and the urge to express the personality of its maker. The first of these should be the concern of painting or music, the second is based on psychological error, since personality, the 'I', is only a broad collective term which embraces the plurality of all the different states of consciousness. Any new state which is added to the others becomes an essential part of this I, and expresses it, whether individually or generally. Any event, any perception, any idea, expresses us with equal power, it can be added to us.... Overcoming this useless and obstinate desire to fix in words a vagabond I, which is transformed every second, Ultraism upholds the central principle of all poetry: to transform the palpable reality of the world into an interior and emotional reality.

In terms of the programme, the argument has moved forward in two ways: it opposes the sensory aspects of *modernismo* and the decadents, and it opposes the emotive nature of late romanticism and the psychologism of the realists and the *naïfs*. Macedonio's definition of art as anti-naturalist is combined with the notion of art as a process. These definitions appeared in all the manifestos of the period and Borges gave them a theoretical density in the first issues of the literary journal *Sur*, in the early 1930s.

As programmes, the theories of the avant-garde could be partially modified in practice. However, their formulations mark out the universe of what is desirable: they operate as true utopias, putting into play, in the literary field, the past, with which they must break, the present, which must be reconstructed in a total way, and the future horizon of the 'new', the attainment of which occupied all their ideological and aesthetic forces. Literary practices found a sense of the future in these excessive and polemical programmes: they offered foundations for transformation.

The utopia of the avant-garde had a force which was not just literary. The manifestos and the polemics stirred up a strong reaction from members of other groups in the intellectual field. These manifestos *are* the avant-garde, as much as the poems themselves, because they demonstrate the absolutist and anti-conciliatory nature of the movement for aesthetic renovation in the 1920s. These manifestos declare: 'We, the young writers, support only "the new" and we will not permit other sectors of society to set the standards for our work.' These writers thus adhered in a radical fashion to the notion of autonomy, stating that the basis of their work was to be found in the work itself, even in work that had not yet been written. They seemed to place themselves outside society, and yet it was society, and their place within it, that made their programme possible. 'The new' was defended precisely by those who were sure of their past, who could refer back to tradition and reaffirm it as if it were a family album. Those who supported the new were not recent arrivals to the country. The recent arrivals, it was felt, defended ethical or ideological principles outside the realms of literature and they needed to establish foundations in order to be accepted as legitimate intellectuals.

The utopia that can be read in these avant-garde programmes functions like all utopias: it expands the limits of the possible, confronting the aesthetic and institutional legitimacy of those who cannot think outside certain well-prescribed limits. Though seeking to free literature from its socio-ideological confines, these avant-garde writers of the 1920s adopted a position far removed from the surrealist project, which took art to the very limits of life. By contrast, this avant-garde separated life and literature, even if a new version of the national question can be read in their texts.

The Case of the Magazine *Proa*

In August 1924, *Proa* was reissued in a new format. On 7 September, *La Nación* mentioned this fact with a careful, or disconcerted, lack of commentary. It reprinted part of *Proa*'s editorial and listed the editors and contributors. When *La Nación* commented on books by the young *ultraistas*, it merely announced that they had been published, and reprinted extracts. Obviously *Proa* presented difficulties for the newspaper because it identified itself as a voice seeking to be heard and understood by its equals and its contemporaries.

The collective text which appears on the first page of the magazine's first issue over the signatures of the editors, Borges, Brandán Caraffa, Güiraldes and Rojas Paz, is a definition of their image, their proposals, their alliances and their hopes. It is a canonical statement which lays out its programme for aesthetic renewal. Conscious of its generational status, the magazine declared that its writers had no truck with the old masters and noted that the First World War had overturned all the old structures and institutions. The war made it 'possible for the first time in this country for a generation to be formed on the margins of the canonical institutions of society'.[9] This attitude would profoundly affect the way in which literary value would be judged, since the magazine did not call upon the great names of the earlier generation to legitimate new writers. Perhaps for the first time in Argentine cultural history, such judgements would be made among equals. The intellectual field was thus split between those who supported change and those who adhered to a continuation of the old order. The first of these groups did not have much power until *Prisma*, *Inicial*, *Martín Fierro* and *Proa* appeared. These magazines and the activities of their contributors gave rise to what Girondo called the 'united front', a focus of intellectual initiatives which also aspired to influence wider currents in Latin America:

> Recently Oliverio Girondo took with him the first fruits of our labour. It had been possible to resolve all the conflicts that had previously separated the main little magazines and form a united front. And Girondo went as an ambassador to try to promote intellectual exchange and to visit the principal Latin American centres of culture.[10]

Proa's mode of presentation offered nothing new: it used ritual formulae of collective identification. Another aspect of this first issue, however, seems more interesting. We find aesthetic and ideological influences in *Proa* which do not appear in *Martín Fierro*: these are the traces of a spirit still influenced by Arielism* and by the new morality among young people which came out of the University Reform, that vast student movement which in 1918 had imposed drastic changes on the teaching system and the running of the university.[11] The editors of *Proa* consider their publication to be part of a 'collective duty' levied on a generation which had been liberated by the war from their mentors and which sought to extend that 'first shaft of illumination, the University Reform'.

Proa, much like the Reform movement, had an outlook characterized by spirituality, by a spirit of renovation and youthfulness. It differs from *Martín Fierro* in that there is no literary feuding in its pages. *Proa* has an explanatory and reasoned tone, although Borges's contributions often display radical and incisive ideas. The moderate style of *Proa* is linked to the reformist tenor of its presentation: the magazine seeks to offer a common, non-sectarian, space.

> We are not trying to lump together diverse groups, undermining different tendencies and smothering different personalities. Our desire is to offer to young writers a serene and unprejudiced forum which will bring together different aspects of mental work that are not purely journalistic.
>
> Our magazine should be of a special kind: neither purely literary nor purely philosophical. Our intelligent young people do not have such a forum, open and without barriers. As a melting-pot of young writers who admire obscure and daily heroism, *Proa* will attempt to mould into an Academy the dispersed energies of a generation that does not feel animosity.[12]

This first text of *Proa* had Arielist echoes and inflections; with its fervour, moral affirmation, seriousness of endeavour, and unity of aspirations, the magazine saw itself as 'a pristine amalgam of dreams and desires'. This Arielist discourse, coupled with ideas from the University Reform, generated a set of appeals and desires which, in 1924, constituted a

---

*The anti-positivist, spiritualist movement that grew up in the River Plate in the first two decades of the century is termed Arielism after the important essay of the Uruguayan José Enrique Rodó, published in 1900. Rodó, making use of the opposition between Shakespeare's Ariel and Caliban, criticized the materialism of local elites and proposed a moral and cultural regeneration based in no small part on the intellectual youth of the continent.

common heritage that could be shared by many of the aesthetic inno-
vators.

This tone united many of the notes and commentaries in the magazine. There was a battle to impose the 'values of the spirit' in a country
whose great men had still not understood these values. The protagonists
of this struggle were young people who hoped for 'a future society where
these values will find a place'.[13]

This same spirit was maintained in subsequent issues. In issue 10, *Proa*
gave three pages over to the news that the Latin-American Union was
being founded. Notes on institutional matters of this kind, especially on
politics, were not frequently published in *Proa*. The Latin-American
Union was an attempt to carry the spirit of the University Reform into a
continental arena. The founders of the Union were writers and young
socialist politicians. Extracts from this declaration, which was outside the
usual preoccupations of *Proa*, give some idea of the climate in which the
magazine appeared. The Union sought

> to develop in the peoples of Latin America a new consciousness of national
> and continental interests, supporting all aspects of the ideological renewal
> which leads to the effective exercise of popular sovereignty, combating any
> dictatorship that might stand in the way of economic reforms inspired by a
> desire for social justice.... Opposition to any financial policies which would
> compromise national sovereignty, and in particular the taking on of any loan
> which might allow or justify the forceful intervention of foreign capital-
> ists.... The nationalization of the sources of wealth and the abolition of
> economic privilege. The struggle against any influence of the Church in
> public life and in education.... The extension of free, secular and compul-
> sory education and an integral university reform.[14]

A mixture of nationalism and spiritualism was sweeping through Latin
America. To what degree can *Proa* be considered part of this climate?
The publication of this document on the foundation of the Latin-
American Union is not enough to settle the point. What it does signify,
however, is a gesture of goodwill towards, and recognition of, currents of
left-democratic and anti-imperialist thought, whose Arielist, spiritualist
and youthful aspects were shared by *Proa*. However, this is not the whole
story. On the one hand, it expressed a desire to map out a common
intellectual field which would encompass all aspects of the avant-garde.
Proa was committed to this in the artistic sphere, whilst recognizing that
other spheres were also legitimate. The experience of the first years of

the avant-garde had shown the need to conquer public spaces; it was possible, therefore, to recognize this same need in the political arena. *Proa* shared with the Reform and the Pan-Latin-American movements the desire to reach a continental audience: the journeys of Oliverio Girondo, the anthologies, the activity of the first years of the literary periodical *Sur* all had the same objective. Furthermore, young people with political involvements tended to filter into the intellectual field, and allegiances were prone to change. The movement for aesthetic reno-vation had not yet become polarized or locked into incompatible ideological positions. On the contrary, in this first half of the 1920s, the 'young' were lined up against the ranks of traditional and well-established intellectuals. It was still a generational movement. In the end, what such overlapping allegiances indicate ia a relatively small intellectual field in which divisions between 'left' and 'right' were less important than those between 'old' and 'new'. There was a shared way of seeing, a shared structure of feeling in the project that sought to conquer society and change it aesthetically, morally or politically. This can be seen in all the editorials published in *Proa*. The magazine tried to compensate for its isolation in a world of large daily newspapers and traditional institutions by calling writers and intellectuals to support different causes and ideas. Issue 11 saw the publication of a letter, signed by Borges, Brandán and Güiraldes, which asked for the support of all writers who approved of the huge ideological and cultural changes which were being set in motion:

> We have hoped, from the beginning, that *Proa* [the 'prow'], living up to its name, should become a rallying point for the struggle, through serious work rather than through mere polemics. We work in the freest but also in the hardest part of the boat, while the literary bourgeoisie sleep in the cabins. From the position we have chosen, we will open up new paths, while they remain behind. Let them call us mad and extravagant. At heart they are tame and will do everything except fight us for the right to work and adventure. Let us be united on this unsteady part of the craft, the part which sets the course. The prow is smaller than the main body of the boat because it is the point where all the energies converge. We laugh at those who rage, since they know that they are born to follow others. Their attacks cannot touch us because they are afraid. *Proa* lives in direct contact with life. It has already been tossed in the waves and is refreshed by optimism and by its desire to conquer distances. Today it wishes to carry on growing. That is why we are writing to you. Give us your strong support to help us guarantee this growth.

Güiraldes is almost certainly responsible for the spiritual tone of such declarations. The young participants of the Reform movement had close (sometimes family) relations with the writers of *Proa*, and the cultivated, creole socialists who signed the Latin-American Union manifesto bore little resemblance to hirsute left militants of immigrant origin. The avant-garde had at the centre of its programme a new-style cultural nationalism. Borges gave it form and tone. Many other articles published in *Proa* share these sentiments but a letter in which the editors declared themselves ready to abandon ship is perhaps the most interesting stylistic example of the blending of the avant-garde and *criollismo*. The letter was sent by Borges to Brandán Caraffa and Ricardo Güiraldes, and it shifts the metaphor from the sea to dry land, to the *orillas*. Its last judgement is criollo as is its paradise:

> ... We will meet again and start up a lively literary gathering, an immortal conversation without ceremony or haste. The patristic tells us little about those friendships at the end of the world, but I think that it is our happy duty to go forward towards this goal, to anticipate God's designs. I cannot think of any endeavour better suited to this purpose than *Proa*.
>
> How splendid are our conversations and discussions! Güiraldes: through the bridge of your austere guitar, through that black hole or window through which we can most certainly glimpse San Antonio de Areco*, far-off places speak to us most eloquently. Brandán seems small, but that is because he is always standing on the other side of one of his verses which have transported him before they carry off the rest of us. Macedonio, behind a cloud of cigarette smoke, that good-natured, creole demigod, knows how to invent a world between two servings of maté tea** and then deflate it again immediately. Rojas Paz, Bernárdez and Marechal almost set the table on fire with their metaphors. Ipuche speaks with a deep voice and is a safe-handed and surefooted messenger, bringing urgent secrets from the forests in Uruguay. Ramos, the Recently-Arrived and the Always-Forewarned† also takes pride of place, and there is a gang of admirable Chileans who have stormed through sandy, distant and humid lands, swept, on occasions, by a black wind, the 'black wind' of Quinto Horacio, that dyer of the sky. There are ten, twenty, thirty of us believing in the possibility of art and friendship. How splendid are our conversations! And yet ... there is a most sacred right

---

*Güiraldes's country house, model for the setting of *Don Segundo Sombra*.
**Maté is most often drunk communally. The gourd is passed around a circle of friends.
†Here Borges is playing with compound adjectives in the style of Macedonio.

in this world: our right to fail, to walk alone and to suffer.... I want to tell you that I am leaving *Proa* and that I am leaving my paper crown on the peg. More than one hundred streets in the *orillas* await me with their moon and solitude and the odd tot of rum. I know that the winds from the pampas are calling Ricardo and the mountains of Córdoba are summoning Brandán. So long, United Front, Ciao Solder, Goodbye all. And Adelina, with that protective grace of yours, give me my coat and stick, because I'm going.[15]

It would be impossible to include more *criollista* references on a single page. *Proa* is coming to an end, Borges writes one of its concluding statements – and carries its poetics to the limits in almost parodic fashion. Obviously a humorous tone dominates in this letter, but it is also important to ask how much truth it tells about *Proa*. Once again its most striking feature is what we have called avant-garde *criollismo*. When, in issue 1 of *Proa*, Borges had written on González Lanuza's *Prismas* (Prisms), he had taken care to differentiate the new Argentine poetics from Spanish Ultraism. The difference lay in the system of reading (which Borges, as usual, falsified), and in the place where the reading was done: under 'the stars of the suburbs'. It is there, precisely, that Borges now placed his literary programme.

> We believe in different things: that the pampa is a shrine; that the first countryman is very much a man; in the strength of the *malevos* (hard men); in the sweet generosity of the *arrabal*. Out of all the limitless riches of the world, what truly belongs to us are the *arrabal* and the *pampa*.[16]

The tango had been banished from the world that 'divine will' created in the suburbs. The creole vanguard could not identify with its music or with lyrics still tainted by crime or by the brothel. For this reason Borges's rereading centred on Carriego (a precursor of the tango to come) and on gauchesque literature. He also highlighted Macedonio's creole inventiveness and it is doubtless true that Macedonio's paradoxes, his 'conceptism' (witty, allusive style), and his plurals* were very much akin to the inventive nature of the *payador*, the gaucho troubadour.

But Borges's version of *criollismo* was not *Proa*'s only programme. As a magazine of the 'united front', it carried out a work of 'pedagogy' by

---

*Macedonio used abstract nouns in the plural, a usage that is not very common in Spanish, but which can be found in the song 'duels' in the poem *Martín Fierro*.

disseminating various tendencies of the European avant-garde. It did this mainly through a series of long articles by Guillermo de Torre who, soon after, would marry the artist Norah Borges, Jorge Luis's sister, who illustrated some issues of *Proa*. Like many of Güiraldes's articles, de Torre's were encyclopaedically up to date but written in a tone that was strangely academic in this world of literary essayists. His notes are explanatory and tend to guide the reader through the new aesthetic principles, rather than vigorously depicting a new field made up of friends and allies. Didactic and somewhat pedantic, these articles of Guillermo de Torre's are an explanatory *vademecum*, a Baedeker to the library shelves. Güiraldes's perceptive review of de Torre's *Literaturas europeas de vanguardia* (Avant-garde European Literatures), points out how the book differs in style and taste from Güiraldes's own work and from that of Borges:

> Guillermo highlights groups and group credos, studying the personalities involved within these broad categories and leaving somewhat to one side isolated individuals whose polemical importance is not so great. This might not be a criterion shared by others who prefer to study works above all as creations of individuals, leaving to one side the historical context of literature and concentrating on its specifically literary nature.[17]

Güiraldes's review underscores the classic contrast between literary history and literature, between productive aesthetic reading and the stolid nature of criticism. His own articles are extremely personal and non-academic essays, usually commentaries on French symbolism and post-symbolism. In one of these articles, on Valéry Larbaud's *A.P. Barnabooth*, Güiraldes offers interesting insights into how he put together his own literary library. Even for a man from a privileged social background such as his, it was a laborious adventure. This is the central theme of the essay: how, in 1919, a friend returning from Europe told him about Larbaud's book, which he obtained only with the greatest difficulty; how he then struck up a personal and literary friendship with Larbaud; and how he found it necessary to break out of the vicious circle of *modernismo*, to overthrow its aesthetic hegemony by introducing other aesthetic principles, and to champion French poets in preference to Darío and Lugones. Even for Güiraldes, this task demanded a firm will and much dedication:

There was a time when it was a great feat to obtain (in Buenos Aires) a book, or even a poem, by the symbolists. However, a handful of young readers, encouraged by the premonitions we had, and guided by a revolutionary obstinacy, managed to make this journey into forbidden territory. In my own case, before people began to laugh at my work, I grew used to them laughing at my choice of reading.... The symbolists were, therefore, our masters.

Rimbaud was so alone that his greatness was chilling.

Mallarmé threw us handfuls of brilliant ideas.

Laforgue seemed to us the one who above all the rest had lived in a state of poetic grace.

Corbière was somewhat different: an anti-literary literature, a pugnacious outward expression of a fierce sensibility wounded by pain.

We had one copy of Isidore Ducasse which we threw at each other's heads, to frighten each other.

Claudel, Verhaeren, those two great figures of neo-symbolism (let us call it that) did not captivate us. Religion, fatherland. We wanted literature above all else. The writer had to show us that art was the core of life.[18]

This was the state of affairs before 1920: an intellectual solitude, as epitomized in Güiraldes, and the search for a new literature, based fundamentally on an aesthetic of renovation. Writing at the time of the Centenario, Lugones had saturated the space of patriotism, and Güiraldes is correct in his intuition that these changes would also affect cultural nationalism. This was the threshold of the establishment of the ideologies of the new. It was necessary to import European writers who could help answer the questions thrown up by the new aesthetic movements and the growing independence of art from social controls. The nature of this importation brought conflict with the *modernistas*, and for this reason *Proa* gave a strategic space and value to the dissemination of foreign authors. This space was substantially different to the classic section 'European literature', which *Nosotros* published efficiently but in an informative rather than a programmatic way. *Proa* made a radical break with such traditionalism by offering, not a showcase of recent publications, but rather a system for understanding the 'new'. It did not give information about all authors or all texts: instead it gave European literature a new function in the context of the River Plate avant-garde.

In the visual arts a similar objective was proposed. Like *Martín Fierro*, *Proa* considered that graphics were important, but it adopted a style which was much less strident than that of *Martín Fierro*, more in keeping with its serious tone. *Proa*'s graphics made great use of vignettes, a great number by Norah Lange and a few from Figari. Number 4 reproduced drawings by Gustav Klimt. The vignettes filled the blank spaces at the bottom of the page, and the spatial layout of the magazine used modern streamlined logotype letters, framed by geometric lines which contrasted sharply with the art deco vignettes and trimmings of the earlier *Proa* magazine. The magazine was thus seen in the same aesthetic frame in which it was read.

Furthermore, in these years, writers and plastic artists were close to each other. The different avant-garde publications stoutly defended the work of the artists Figari and Petorutti. Graphics is like translation: it is a visual demonstration of the magazine's point of view, from the moment when the readers first leaf through the text. *Martín Fierro* altered the traditional format of the page, while *Proa* showed its commitment to the principles of a more moderate aesthetic modernity. The avant-garde writers did not believe that graphics usurped a space which should be filled wholly by writing; they were not economical, and indeed had no reason to be.

If there was a policy towards graphic art, there was also a move to instigate what Borges calls 'a politics of language'.[19] What did this mean? And why was it necessary? Both Borges and González Lanuza in these years experimented with orthography.[20] The manifesto–proclamation of *Prisma* was written according to the new rules that Borges would use in his first books. Spelling reform can be seen as playing an important part in the project of the avant-garde even though only a couple of writers fleetingly adopted it. It implied a break with academic norms and it fuelled the debate between the avant-garde and Spain which broke out in *Martín Fierro*, as we have seen, when Madrid was proposed as the 'cultural meridian' of Latin America and Borges demolished the idea in his reply to Américo Castro. But more important is the fact that this *porteño* spelling was a refutation of linguistic norms that paralleled poetry's refutation of the norms of prosody. It had ideological and aesthetic connotations because it represented — graphically — the River Plate's urban oral language, which Borges was working on at that time. It became an instantly recognizable gesture for it was not necessary to read the texts to note these changes: it was enough to see them in their graphic form. This project, furthermore, was carried out by writers who were as sure of their phonetics as they were of their origins. Such behaviour would have been unthinkable among the recent arrivals on the intellectual scene, who were unsure of their spelling, or among those for whom the acquisition of writing had been a recent and painful process. As in the work of Sarmiento, the reform of spelling is utopian and radical, indicating the depth and extent of other changes in style, form and prosody. It did not offer a mimetic transcription of oral language, but rather a refutation of norms at all levels.

The problem of language was central to the Argentine avant-garde, in the first place because it was a central problem of the wider society: language seemed uncertain not for reasons of excessive linguistic purity but because Buenos Aires had in recent decades become a free port for immigrants. Even the intellectual field was made up of voices that did not share the linguistic register, acquired over many years, of the old criollos. Other phonetic inflections were jostling for space and corrupting literature. Borges was an ironic participant in this debate with the purists, for he too, after his fashion, opposed *lunfardo* (urban argot), which he considered to be a hybrid of the suburbs and immigration:

> But it is necessary to differentiate between outward and essential riches. A man uses the correct, latinate term *prostituta* (prostitute). The dictionary immediately falls on his head, silencing him with words such as *meretriz* and *buscona.** The neighbourhood tough will add words such as *yiro, yiradora, turra, mina, milonga.*** This does not demonstrate the richness of our language. It is, rather, showy demonstrativeness — since this junkyard of words does not help us to feel or to think.[21]

This text of Borges's demonstrates his own use of language, one of the great inventions of the period: *'se le viene encima'*, ('fall on his head'), *'le tapa la boca'* ('silence him', literally 'closing his mouth'), *farolería*, ('showy demonstrativeness') and *cambalache* ('junkyard') are all words or expressions taken from River Plate colloquial Spanish. Borges is here making literary language criollo, one of the riskiest undertakings possible if we consider the attempts at criollo literature previously seen in Argentina. Borges's 'creolization' is permanently pushing at the limits: it introduces lexical and syntactical changes, but above all it affects the rhythm of the period and of the sentence. It is not ostensibly lexical, because Borges

---

* 'literary' words for prostitute.
** *lunfardo* or urban slang words meaning 'street walking', 'street walker', 'easy lay', 'doll', 'milonga' (a song and dance form).

avoids *lunfardo* and gauchesque terms, choosing instead a corpus of words with blurred contours, and expressions which can sometimes be traced back to the gauchesque but which can almost always be found in the spoken language of urban criollos of long standing. The corpus is familiar and masculine, never vulgar or plebeian.

A politics of language is based on the conviction that this language is a historic and modifiable instrument which can therefore both resist the system and offer a canvas on which to place the imprints of a sensibility and of a nation:

> What I hope to do is awaken in each writer the realization that the potential of languages is scarcely being tapped and that the glory and duty of all of us lies in multiplying and varying it. Every literary generation that is awake has understood this fact.[22]

A linguistic imagination pervaded these works of Borges and informed his readings of gauchesque literature, which appeared in *Proa* and later in *Sur*. His was an imagination as opposed to the sinuous tradition of the *modernistas* as to the anti-poetic literalness of the language of left-wing humanitarian writers. This linguistic imagination leapt backwards and sideways with a freedom that only the avant-garde could have produced: towards the gauchesque, towards the old criollo traditions, towards the inflections of plain and trivial oral language. Cultural nationalism was thus given a new formal and aesthetic definition by the avant-garde of the 1920s. And the literary imagination, free at last from *modernismo*, redefined the space of Argentine letters.

Notes

1. Néstor Ibarra, *La nueva poesía argentina*, Buenos Aires 1930, pp. 15-16.
2. Ibid., p. 21.
3. *Poesía*, 1-2, 1933, p. 43.
4. *Simplismo: poemas inventados por Alberto Hidalgo*, Buenos Aires 1925, p. 13.
5. Prologue to *La roas blindada* (1936), quoted in the Horizonte edition, Buenos Aires 1962.
6. *La nueva poesía argentina*, p. 127.
7. Vicente Huidobro, *Obras completas*, Santiago de Chile 1964, p. 686. On Huidobro, see George Yúdice, *Vicente Huidobro y la motivación del lenguaje*, Buenos Aires 1978.
8. *Anatomía de mi Ultra*, text of 1921, quoted in César Fernández Moreno, *La realidad y los papeles*, Madrid 1967, p. 493.

9. *Proa*, 1, p. 40.

10. Ibid., pp. 4–5.

11. Raul Crisafio notes: 'The new poetics was drastically opposed to 'commercial' society. And it opposed this society by using, on more than one occasion, ideas and feelings that were present in the University Reform of 1918 ... demanding the destruction of anachronistic, parasitic and traditional institutions and denouncing the acquiescence of the population in the daily routine and the consequent rejection of anything new.' 'Boedo-Florida e la letterature argentina degli anni venti', *Materiali Critici* (Geneva), 2, 1981, p. 374. Maria Luisa Bastos also points out these stylistic traces in *Inicial*: see her *Borges ante la crítica argentina 1923–1960*, Buenos Aires 1974, pp. 24, 25 and 38.

12. *Proa*, 1, pp. 4–6.

13. Unsigned commentary on the 'Amigos del Arte' Association, *Proa*, 1, p. 28.

14. *Proa*, 10, pp. 65–6.

15. Letter dated 1 July 1925 and published in *Proa*, 15, pp. 26–7.

16. 'La pampa y el suburbio son dioses', *Proa*, no. 15.

17. *Proa*, 8, p. 15.

18. 'Un libro', *Proa*, 3, pp. 35–6.

19. 'El idioma infinito', *Proa*, no. 12.

20. The omission of the 'd' at the end of a word; the use of i instead of y in conjunctions and at the end of a word with a diphthong; an erratic, but irreverent use of j and g.

21. 'El idioma infinito', p. 43.

22. Ibid., p. 46.

Bibliography

Works by J.L. Borges

Dates correspond to first editions.

1923   *Fervor de Buenos Aires*, Buenos Aires.
1925   *Luna de enfrente*, Buenos Aires.
1925   *Inquisiciones*, Buenos Aires.
1926   *El tamaño de mi esperanza*, Buenos Aires.
1928   *El idioma de los argentinos*, Buenos Aires.
1929   *Cuaderno San Martín*, Buenos Aires.
1930   *Evaristo Carriego*, Buenos Aires.
1932   *Discusión*, Buenos Aires.
1935   *Historia universal de la infamia*, Buenos Aires.
1936   *Historia de la eternidad*, Buenos Aires.
1940   *Antología de la literatura fantástica* (with Silvina Ocampo and Adolfo Bioy Casares), Buenos Aires.
1941   *El jardín de los senderos que se bifurcan*, Buenos Aires.
1942   *Seis problemas para don Isidro Parodi* (with A. Bioy Casares), Buenos Aires.
1943   *Poemas 1922–1943*, Buenos Aires.
1944   *Artificios*, Buenos Aires.
1944   *Ficciones (1935–1944)*, Buenos Aires.
1949   *El Aleph*, Buenos Aires.
1951   *La muerte y la brújula*, Buenos Aires.
1952   *Otras inquisiciones*, Buenos Aires.
1953   *El 'Martín Fierro'*, Buenos Aires.

1958   *Poemas (1923–1958)*, Buenos Aires.
1960   *El hacedor*, Buenos Aires.
1963   *El lenguaje de Buenos Aires*, Buenos Aires.
1964   *El otro, el mismo*, Buenos Aires.
1964   *Obra poética (1923–1964)*, Buenos Aires.
1965   *Para las seis cuerdas*, Buenos Aires.
1967   *Crónicas de Bustos Domecq* (with A. Bioy Casares), Buenos Aires.
1969   *Elogio de la sombra*, Buenos Aires.
1970   *El informe de Brodie*, Buenos Aires.
1972   *El oro de los tigres*, Buenos Aires.
1974   *Obras completas, 1923–1972*, Buenos Aires.
1975   *El libro de arena*, Buenos Aires.
1975   *La rosa profunda*, Buenos Aires.
1975   *Prólogos. Con un prólogo de prólogos*, Buenos Aires.
1976   *La moneda de hierro*, Buenos Aires.
1976   *Cosmogonías*, Buenos Aires.
1977   *Rosa y azul*, Barcelona.
1977   *Historia de la noche*, Buenos Aires.
1978   *El libro de los seres imaginarios*, Buenos Aires.
1979   *Borges oral*, Buenos Aires.
1980   *Siete noches*, Mexico City.
1981   *La cifra*, Buenos Aires.
1982   *Nueve ensayos dantescos*, Madrid.
1985   *Los conjurados*, Madrid.
1986   *Atlas*, Barcelona.
1986   *Textos cautivos* (edited by E. Sacerio Gari and E. Rodriguez Monegal), Barcelona.

English Translations

Publication details are taken from Jason Wilson, *An A to Z of Modern Latin American Literature in English Translation*, Institute of Latin American Studies, London, 1989, pp. 20–22.

Labyrinths: Selected Stories and Other Writings, New York 1962; Harmondsworth 1970.
Ficciones, New York 1962; London, 1962; also published as *Fictions*, London 1965.
Other Inquisitions, Austin (Texas) 1964; New York 1965; London 1973.
Dreamtigers, Univ. of Texas Press: Austin (Texas) 1964; London, 1973.
A Personal Anthology, New York 1967; London 1968.

The Book of Imaginary Beings (with Margarita Guerrero), New York 1969; London, 1970.
The Aleph and Other Stories, 1933–1969, New York 1970; London 1971.
Extraordinary Tales (with Adolfo Bioy Casares), New York 1971; London 1973.
An Introduction to American Literature (with Esther Zemborain de Torres), Lexington (Kentucky) 1971.
Selected Poems (1923–1967), New York 1972; Harmondsworth 1972.
A Universal History of Infamy, New York 1972; London 1973.
Doctor Brodie's Report, New York 1972; Harmondsworth 1974.
The Congress London, 1973.
In Praise of Darkness, New York 1974; London 1975.
Introduction to English Literature (with María Esther Vásquez), London 1975.
Chronicles of Bustos Domecq (with Adolfo Bioy Casares), New York 1976; London 1982.
The Gold of the Tigers: Selected Later Poems, New York 1977.
The Book of Sand, New York 1977; London 1979.
Six Problems for Don Isidro Parodi (with Adolfo Bioy Casares), New York 1981; London 1981.
Borges: A Reader. A Selection from the Writings of Jorge Luis Borges, New York 1981.
Evaristo Carriego, New York 1984.
Seven Nights, New York 1984; London 1986.
Atlas (with María Kodoma), New York 1985; London 1986.

Selected Works on J.L. Borges

Jaime Alazraki, *La prosa narrativa de Jorge Luis Borges,* Madrid 1968.
—— *Jorge Luis Borges,* New York 1971.
—— *Versiones, inversiones, reversiones,* Madrid 1977.
—— (ed.) *Critical Essays on Jorge Luis Borges,* Boston 1987.
Daniel Balderston, *El precursor velado: R.L. Stevenson en la obra de Borges,* Buenos Aires 1985.
—— *The Literary Universe of Jorge Luis Borges,* New York 1986.
Ana María Barrenechea, *La expresión de la irrealidad en la obra de Jorge Luis Borges,* Buenos Aires 1967.
Willis Barnstone, *Borges at Eighty: Conversations,* Bloomington (Indiana) 1982.
María Luisa Bastos, *Borges ante la crítica argentina,* Buenos Aires 1974.
Gene Bell-Villada, *Borges and His Fiction: A Guide to His Mind and Art,* Chapel Hill (N. Carolina) 1981.
Harold Bloom, ed., *Jorge Luis Borges,* New York 1986.
Richard Burgin, *Conversations with Jorge Luis Borges,* New York 1970.

BIBLIOGRAPHY

Roger Caillois, 'Postface du traducteur', in Jorge Luis Borges, *Histoire de l'infamie/Histoire de l'éternité*, Paris 1964.

Michael Capobianco, 'Mathematics in the "Ficciones" of Jorge Luis Borges', *International Fiction Review*, Winter 1982.

Cleon Wade Capsus, *The Poetry of Jorge Luis Borges*, New Mexico 1964.

Serge Champeau, *Borges et la métaphysique*, Paris 1990.

Georges Charbonnier, *Entretiens avec J.L. Borges*, Paris 1967.

Ronald Christ, *The Narrow Act: Borges' Art of Allusion*, New York 1969.

David Cohen, *An Introduction to Borges' Labyrinths*, Boston 1970.

John Alexander Coleman, 'Notes on Borges and American Literature', *Tri-Quarterly*, no. 25, 1972.

Edgardo Cozarinsky, *Borges y el cine*, Buenos Aires 1974.

Cuarenta inquisiciones sobre Borges, *Revista Iberoamericana*, special issue, vol. 43, no. 100–101, 1977.

Giovanna De Garayalde, *Jorge Luis Borges: Sources and Illumination*, London 1979.

Albert Devran, *Borges et la Kabbale*, Brussels 1967.

Arturo Echevarría, *Lengua y literatura de Borges*, Barcelona 1983.

César Fernández Moreno, *Esquema de Borges*, Buenos Aires 1957.

Osvaldo Ferrari, *Libro de diálogos*, Buenos Aires 1986.

Angel Flores, ed., *Expliquemos a Borges como poeta*, Mexico City 1984.

David William Foster, *Jorge Luis Borges. An Annotated Primary and Secondary Bibliography*, New York 1984.

Zunilda Gertel, *Borges y su retorno a la poesía*, New York 1967.

Gerardo Goloboff, *Leer Borges*, Buenos Aires 1978.

Cristina Grau, *Borges y la arquitectura*, Madrid 1989.

Rafael Gutiérrez Girardot, *Jorge Luis Borges: ensayo de interpretación*, Madrid 1959.

James Irby, 'Borges and the Idea of Utopia', *Books Abroad*, vol. 45, no. 3, 1971.

—— 'Introduction', *Labyrinths*, Harmondsworth 1970.

—— *The Structure of the Stories of J.L. Borges*, Michigan 1963.

James Irby, Napoleón Murat, Carlos Peralta, *Encuentro con Borges*, Buenos Aires 1968.

Alicia Jurado, *Genio y figura de Jorge Luis Borges*, Buenos Aires 1964.

John King, '"A Curiously Colonial Performance": The Eccentric Vision of V.S. Naipaul and J.L. Borges', *The Yearbook of English Studies*, vol. 13, 1983.

L'Herne, special issue on Jorge Luis Borges, Paris 1964.

Robert Lima, ed., *Borges the Labyrinth Maker*, New York 1965.

Gabriela Massuh, *Borges: una estética del silencio*, Buenos Aires 1980.

Blas Matamoro, *Jorge Luis Borges o el juego trascendente*, Buenos Aires 1980.

Jean de Milleret, *Entretiens avec J.L. Borges*, Paris 1967.

Sylvia Molloy, *Las letras de Borges*, Buenos Aires 1979.

Juan Nuño, *La filosofía de Borges*, Mexico City 1987.
Victoria Ocampo, *Diálogo con Borges*, Buenos Aires 1969.
Roberto Paoli, *Borges. Percorsi di significato*, Florence 1977.
Alberto Julián Pérez, *Poética de la prosa de J.L. Borges*, Madrid 1986.
Enrique Pezzoni, *El texto y sus voces*, Buenos Aires 1989.
Adolfo Prieto, *Borges y la nueva generación*, Buenos Aires 1954.
—— *Prose for Borges*, Evanston (Illinois) 1974.
Jaime Rest, *El laberinto del universo*, Buenos Aires 1976.
Emir Rodríguez Monegal, *Borges: hacia una interpretación*, Madrid 1976.
—— *Borges par lui-même*, Paris 1970.
—— *Jorge Luis Borges: A Literary Biography*, New York 1978.
Martin Stabb, *Jorge Luis Borges*, New York 1970.
Saúl Sosnowski, *Borges y la cábala: la búsqueda del verbo*, Buenos Aires 1976.
John Sturrock, *Paper Tigers: The Ideal Fictions of Jorge Luis Borges*, Oxford 1977.
María Esther Vázquez, *Borges: imágenes, memorias, diálogos*, Caracas 1977.
Cesco Vian, *Invito alla lettura di Jorge Luis Borges*, Milan 1980.
Carter Wheelock, *The Mythmaker: A Study of Motif and Symbol in the Short Stories of Jorge Luis Borges*, Austin (Texas) 1969.
Saul Yurkievich, *Fundadores de la nueva poesía latinoamericana*, Barcelona 1971.

INDEX